The Soul Garden Pathway

Discovery Guide

Sally Gallot-Reeves

Balboa Press books may be ordered through booksellers or by contacting:

Balboa Press
A Division of Hay House
1663 Liberty Drive
Bloomington, IN 47403
www.balboapress.com
844-682-1282

Because of the dynamic nature of the Internet, any web addresses or links contained in this book may have changed since publication and may no longer be valid. The views expressed in this work are solely those of the author and do not necessarily reflect the views of the publisher, and the publisher hereby disclaims any responsibility for them.

Any people depicted in stock imagery provided by Getty Images are models, and such images are being used for illustrative purposes only.
Certain stock imagery © Getty Images.

Cover Art by
Linde Mills Art, Knoxville, Tennessee
lindemillsart@gmail.com

Author photography by
Ron St. Jean Photography
Dover, NH 03820
www.ronstjeanphotography.com

ISBN: 978-1-9822-6213-6 (sc)
ISBN: 978-1-9822-6214-3 (e)

Library of Congress Control Number: 2021900985

Print information available on the last page.

Balboa Press rev. date: 05/12/2021

BALBOA.PRESS
A DIVISION OF HAY HOUSE

The kiss of the sun
for pardon,
The song of the birds
for mirth.
One is nearer to God's heart
in a garden
Than anywhere else on earth.

Dorothy Frances Gurney
From the poem, The Lord God Planted a Garden

ACKNOWLEDGEMENTS

My heart speaks with overflowing *Gratitude* ....

For my Divine Calling which energizes and sustains me, and urges me forward.

For the angelic realm and my celestial guides whose abundant messages, wisdom, and enlightenment encouraged me to translate into words the dimensions of spiritual oneness within me and all of us, in Light and Love.

For my dear family and friends throughout the world who surround me with pure unconditional love, inner peace, and belief in my becoming and sharing... *more.*

For the *aunts:* Ruth, Barbara, Rose and Anne. Your generosities of lovingkindness continue to light the candle of my heart.

For spiritual mentors and energy healers; Carolyn A. Jones, The Energy Architect, and Hilary McCann Crowley, Energy Medicine Practitioner.

For Candace S. Smith, PhD, RN, for embracing my daily blessings of love that planted a seed, which grew above and below, and flourished into a beautiful Soul Garden of faith, compassion, and hopefulness for all.

For all soul sister nurses, one with me in mind~body~spirit. For your giving hearts and caring souls. You make a difference in the lives of many every day.

For dedicated artists, Janet Edkins and Linde Mills. For your friendship, patience, and creativity in making the Soul Garden Pathway and website a unique and beautiful opus for all to share.

For all supporters and transcendent influencers who share in prayer to help heal the planet spiritually, emotionally, and physically. You are truly blessed and blessing the world.

For the gifts of the abundant Universe. For all who have come before me, are with me, and will find me.... whose minds are one with all minds in blessed purpose every day. May all be blessed.

~ Dear Lord, may I see that I am becoming whole in your eyes.
May I see that I am part of the whole in mine ~
Sally Gallot-Reeves
Spiritual Gardener, author

INTRODUCTION

*"We are not human beings having a spiritual experience.
We are spiritual beings having a human experience."*
Pierre Teilhard de Chardin
French philosopher, Jesuit Priest

When I first read The Soul Garden Pathway I thought, "This is it! This is the guidebook that weaves the internal experience with the external experience of life and allows the individual to understand what is often presented as complicated esoteric concepts in an understandable way."

It is a guidebook that can be heard through the heart and understood through the mind. As an intuitive channel and healer, I have often found in my work that blending the head and heart energies together is one of the greatest journeys. This is the perfect tool to facilitate just that.

The Soul Garden Pathway is a self-expansive masterpiece encoded with love and light in every written word. It has been written to assist the reader to find the soul garden that lies within each of us and is connected to our own individualized Tree of Life.

The Tree of Life has various meanings in different cultures and religions and I believe them to be the key to self-mastery and enlightenment. By working through the energy centers of the body and mastering the lower energies of the self we are able to expand beyond any preconceived thoughts of our own existence. In doing so, one is able to explore the higher states of consciousness that exist for all those that wish to engage. It allows for the discovery of peace and serenity that lies deep within the heart chakra underneath the many layers of energy and conditioning.

It is a resource, a tool, and a roadmap that allows the reader to look deep within and discover that which has been hidden right before their very eyes their whole life... themselves.

The Soul Garden Pathway, is woven like a tapestry of the phases and seasons of life and it is designed for both those that are newly awakened on their spiritual journey and for those that are already awakened looking to expand further.

I found it to be a journey of the self within the Self and if the reader allows, the pathway will lead them back home. They will have the opportunity to step into who they came here to be outside of the emotional, mental, spiritual and physical stages of human conditioning and limitations.

As we move more into the unknowns of life, it is absolutely crucial to have connection with our Higher Self as a guidepost along our journey to navigate the ever changing energies and circumstances coming our way. The Soul Garden opens the door and expands the awareness of the internal workings of our being. We are given the opportunity to explore our internal

garden as a landscape of mass potentiality while simultaneously accessing multidimensional states of consciousness and truths.

Soul Garden has a unique way of exploring the inner workings of the soul from seedling to a mature tree. It will shift, expand and enhance your thinking in a way you never thought possible. It will provide you with insight, guidance and direction. It will shine the light on the shadow within so that it may be healed and integrated into the whole being.

Using the Guidebook empowers you to discover what stands in your way of healing the distortions of your life whether it be lack of self-love, self-nurturance, the wounded child within or the shadow aspects of the psyche. You have the opportunity to shift your perspective to look at everything that has occurred in your life and all that is occurring in a brand new way supporting your expansion out of victim consciousness.

Flow in Divine Energy as you journey through the Soul Garden. Weed out the energy that no longer serves you so that you can create more space within the garden of your soul. This will allow more seedlings to be planted for new growth.

Give yourself the opportunity to expand and look within to see areas of your life that can be re-examined and re-evaluated so that you may come into a higher understanding of your role in the Universe.

Utilize the inquiries, exercises and thought provoking discovery questions that serve as a tool throughout the book. They will help you determine where you want to focus your energy and what you wish to manifest and bring forth in your life.

Wherever you are in life and whatever stage, enjoy this beautiful guidebook while you expand on your journey exploring the seasons of life in and the inner workings of your soul.

Carolyn A. Jones, The Energy Architect™
The Holistic Institute of Wellness
HolisticInstituteofWellness.com

TABLE OF CONTENTS

PREFACE

Awaken every given day to Divine Light and listen to the messages from within ....

Beyond the physicality of ourselves we search for a place of peace, a place of rest and reflection that illuminates the meaning of our life. A sacred place that allows us to be and see our true selves without judgment, as spiritual beings in human form.

It is not in our minds.

The Soul Garden lies within our hearts and higher self, one with spirit.

A space wherein we are whole, accepted, loved, and supported at all times and in all we do. Unique to each of us, the Garden is a sanctum, a place of limitless thought and freedom, opportunity and peace; a perfect blending and balance of all there is, all that has been, and all that will be.

Your Soul Garden, the Sanctuary of Your Soul, has existed throughout time, not to be created but to be found. A mystery not to unravel, but to unveil.

Come walk with me on the golden pathway from your heart to the spiritual soul garden of serenity, understanding, and oneness with all there is.

~ May your journey be blessed with discovery and truth ~
Sally Gallot-Reeves
Spiritual Gardener, author
Soulgardenpathway.com

CHAPTER 1

The Passageway

Relax into your physical being....
Open your mind and consciously breathe. Allow your breaths to flow within you and through you. Deep breaths of life into your heart.
The passageway opens, beckoning and enticing you forward to explore, to learn, to grow.
This is your journey of discovery and enlightenment.

Life Began in a Garden...

> ~ *We cannot kindle when we will*
> *The fire in the heart resides*
> *The spirit bloweth and is still*
> *In mystery our soul abides* ~
> Matthew Arnold
> British Poet

"Life began in a garden" as the story of Adam and Eve depicts, reflects an abundant haven that was rejected by man and woman through sin, through their freedom of choice. Our Soul Garden is the creation of ourselves, our higher self and spirit, a place where our choices are capable of creating abundance. In the garden we are always whole, always bringing into being the life we are designed to have, the life that serves our purpose. Our Soul Garden is vibrantly alive with living energy along the paths we walk; past, present and future.

Abundance is a perception of wholeness in our lives. A feeling that everything we need and desire is available to us. We are free from worry and want. In the physical world, abundance is associated with security. In the spiritual world, abundance is associated with limitless creativity. Abundance exists in all of us, at all times, and in multiple forms. It is readily available to be accessed.

> ~ *Creation is only the projection into form of that which already exists* ~
> Shrimad Bhagavatan
> from the ancient Vedic Literature

As we progress into Discovery Thoughts, questions which help you to assimilate and process what you have read, consider how they relate to yourself, life circumstances and experiences. What feelings, memories and emotions are kindled? What are you grateful and thankful for? What would you like to recreate? Remember that what is within one, is also created in the whole.

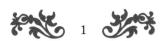

Discovery Thought....

Take a moment and reflect on the abundance in your life. What things represent security? What things represent limitless creativity?

_____
_____
_____
_____
_____
_____
_____
_____
_____
_____
_____

What are you grateful for? Why?

_____
_____
_____
_____
_____
_____
_____
_____
_____
_____
_____
_____
_____
_____

Affirmations are conscious positive statements that reinforce our thinking. They set an intention, influencing the thoughts of the subconscious and conscious mind. Affirmations align the physical being [body/mind] with the Higher Self [spirit], and project positive energy out into the universe to be acted upon.

Affirmation: I am a dynamic source of limitless abundance. I create what I desire.
Please add an affirmative thought to continue your flow of positive energy
I..._____

As human beings in spiritual form, Homo Luminous, (a human being of light), we are designed in Divine Likeness and then develop components and characteristics that make us unique

individuals. Your soul is seeded in a physical vessel that expands in three dimensions, Mind, Body, and Spirit.

> ~ *Since you are like no other being ever created since the*
> *beginning of time, you are incomparable* ~
> Brenda Ueland
> Journalist and teacher

You are capable of receiving and creating vibrational energy to manifest thoughts into a tangible reality. You are a life giving form of the universe, blessed with guidance and intuitive wisdom, and responsible for your acts. This awareness brings immense opportunity and gifts into your life for you to utilize as you desire.

Think about your soul garden. A beautiful place of expanding life. When we tend our soul garden abundance blooms from every plant and tree. Tended with gratitude and love, what we think, feel, and say recreates in a living form following the Universal Law of Cause and Effect. New life flourishes from our actions.

Know that you are blessed to create on earth the garden which is mirrored in your soul. You are empowered by Divine Light and Love.

Discovery Thought....
Picture your soul garden, your place of love and serenity. What do you see? Breathe in the aroma of blossoms. What do you feel?

_____

_____

_____

_____

_____

_____

_____

_____

_____

_____

_____

_____

_____

_____

Affirmation: I am the beauty of my soul. I bloom with generosity, kindness, and love.
Please add an affirmative thought to continue your flow of positive energy
I....._____

> ~ *The life we want is not merely the one we have chosen and made.*
> *It is the one we must be choosing and making* ~
> Wendell Berry
> American novelist, poet and activist

As you are reading this, you are using the skills of your mind, the bountiful gifts of cognitive development, thinking and interpretation. The human mind believes that by using logic the underlying purpose of life is understood, but it is by loving acceptance of all experiences that our journeys gain trajectory. Credence opens us to the flow of universal energy and direction while our life purpose is an ever evolving process of discovery.

Many of us search for meaning beyond our everyday lives. The source of things we cannot explain and the unexpected occurrences in our life. Life forces innately draw us to our place of origin, the ethereal plane. Behind the veil, the universe seeks to connect us to where we are from, assist us to determine where we are, and help us choose how to move forward.

Our sacred soul is eternal, transcending time, and choosing to live temporarily in a physical vessel to bring Divine Purpose, Light and Love into the world. On earth we are blessed by grace, benevolence, and faith that nurtures and liberates us. We embrace peace, harmony and balance to thrive within challenging and harsh environments. By our thoughts, words and actions we continue to create our Soul Garden.

You... you are your soul garden. You are the energetic manifestation of your gifts and the spiritual light you bring into the world. What you desire is the discovery of yourself. Journey inward...

The Tree of Life

> ~ *Only when inspired to go beyond consciousness by some*
> *extraordinary insight does beauty manifest unexpectedly* ~
> Arthur Erickson
> Canadian architect and urban planner

You are able to enter your soul garden through your heart. Place your hands, left over right, in the center of your chest and begin to take some slow deep breaths..... in and out ...... slow deep breaths... as you begin to visualize this sacred place. It breathes with you. It is filled with beauty and light so limitless it is beyond your sight.

In your soul garden growth occurs in all directions in living, vibrating energy. As you walk forward you are bathed in golden yellow light, a light that guides you. In the center stands a majestic tree, your tree of life, rooted deeply into the vastness of the earth and reaching upward to the heavenly realms. Your tree of life is a symbol of your lives on earth expressed in the fundamental principles of nature and the connective relationships between mind~body~spirit.

The Tree of Life has been written about for centuries. To the ancient Egyptians, the Tree of Life represented the hierarchical chain of events that brought everything into existence. The core rings, or spheres, demonstrated the order, process, and method of creation.

In Buddhism, the Tree of Life is known as the Bhodi-tree, the tree of enlightenment, under which Buddha received his gifts of knowledge and understanding.

And in the Book of Genesis in the Bible, the Tree of Life [the tree of knowledge] grew within the Garden of Eden and was considered the source of eternal life.

∿ To put it in a modern way, Karma can be explained as the tendencies of the soul, because Karma is the imprint of the memories from past lives that remain in each soul ∿
Buddha
Spiritual teacher, philosopher

The Tree of Life also embodies karma, the sum of a person's actions in this and previous states of existence which is transferred by their soul through all lifetimes. As a result of past experiences and their outcomes, Karma that we embody influences us. In the present lifetime we are also creating new karma by continuing to make choices and respond to experiences. Being present, being aware and conscious of our actions, is key to owning the responsibility of who we are and who we want to be.

Consider the magnitude of karma as an energy force. Consider its role and purpose in our Tree of Life. Karma brings openings for awareness and insight into our lives. The gift of karma allows us to reexamine and make changes in our life that create new direction and new life purpose.

Discovery Thought....
As you continue to make choices in your life, how do past experiences influence you?

_____

_____

_____

_____

_____

_____

_____

_____

_____

_____

_____

_____

_____

_____

_____

Physical, psychological, economic, and environmental factors create our outer world. How do you feel they impact your ability to live life fully?

_____
_____
_____
_____
_____
_____
_____
_____
_____
_____
_____
_____
_____
_____

Affirmation: My life is blessed with Karmic insight.
I make decisions for my highest good as I live in the present.
Please add an affirmative thought to continue your flow of positive energy
I....._____

"All theory, dear friend, is gray, but the golden tree of life springs ever green."
Johann Wolfgang von Goethe
German author, scientist

Consider the Tree of Life.... you, in all of your magnificent aspects...

Trees have heritage, life line and ancestry. They are reflective of past and present and give promise to what can be created in the future. They are alive! At the center of your soul garden your Tree of Life grows in Divine Light as the focal point of all of your existence.

Roots – Life Giving

~ *God Bless the Roots! Body and Soul are one* ~
Theodore Roethke
American poet

The roots of the Tree of Life Represent your Body, the physical vessel, anchored in the earth. Beginning with the emergence of your ethereal seed, germination begins and heralds the process of coming into existence, growth, and development.

Roots lie in two planes, connecting beneath the soil and above the soil, providing connections to your past and present. It is frequently noted, "as above, so below", and with this bilevel symmetry we can grow again in multiple dimensions.

Roots provide structure, support, and absorption. They balance all that grows above it and allow us to ground energy back into the earth, to Mother Earth, to nourish and bless it. The Self is reborn each year with the enlargement of tree roots that bring fresh opportunity into the garden and our lives.

Trunk – Life Connecting

~ *Thinkers, listen, tell me what you know of that is not inside the soul?* ~
Kabir
Indian mystic, poet and saint

The trunk of the Tree of Life Represents your Spirit, the energy communicator between all dimensions. Breathing inward and outward with palpable vibration, the tree exchanges vital nutrients to enrich the environment and itself. Energy is its lifeline.

The trunk transports messages to roots and branches and influences involuntary functions as it grows; ensuring we strive to our maximal potential. Within the trunk, rings are a manifestation of growth years and lifetimes. The internal core protects the vein, our heart connection and communicator to Physical, to Mind, and to our Higher Self/Spirit.

The Tree of Life allows us to be a conduit from heaven to earth, from spirit to form.

Branches – Life Attaining

~ Choice confers freedom – the freedom to embrace the new
because it speaks to your soul and you are listening ~
Sarah Ban Breathnach
Author, philanthropist

The multiple branches of the Tree of Life <u>Represent your Mind</u>, connecting you to the world, the universe, and all of nature. Visually branching into stems and leaves, they symbolize our actions on three levels:

- The creation of thoughts, perceptions, and understandings
- The incorporation of knowledge, wisdom, and emotions
- The choices we make, the growth we incur, the impact we have on ourselves and others

Our branches are functional in every season, providing new growth in the spring, shade in the heat of summer, harvest of the fruits of fall, and openings for light to pass in the dark days of winter. Through branching we gain earthly and spiritual clarity that provides a platform from which to grow again.

The Tree of Life Encompasses Mind~Body~Spirit…..

Roots represent the body, anchored in the earth and connecting upward to the trunk, your spirit self. Communicating below and above, the spirit trunk is your core balance in life and assists your branches in determining choices and experiences. The energy you absorb, transmit, and release is reflected in your growth.

The Tree of Life is a miracle of creation from inception, just as you are. Consider how expertly and meaningfully connected all components are designed and function. Looking at its majesty, we experience thankfulness and gratitude for our life, for all lives, for all that has been, is present, and will be. We know we are Divinely inspired and the purpose and intention of our lives is far greater than we are able to comprehend.

~ Gratitude unlocks the fullness of life.
It turns what we have into enough, and more.
It turns denial into acceptance, chaos into order, confusion into clarity……
Gratitude makes sense of our past, brings peace for today, and creates a vision
for tomorrow~
Melody Beattie
American author, self-help blogger

Discovery Thought....

Visualize your Tree of Life. What physical qualities are contained within the roots? How do you nourish yourself and the earth?

_____
_____
_____
_____
_____
_____
_____
_____
_____
_____
_____
_____

The trunk of the tree is your spiritual communicator. How does spiritual energy connect with your physical being, body and mind?

_____
_____
_____
_____
_____
_____
_____
_____
_____
_____
_____
_____

Your branches represent your mind. Look at how they reach out into the world. What are you reaching for? What are you searching for?

_____
_____
_____
_____

_____

_____

_____

_____

_____

_____

_____

_____

_____

_____

Affirmation: I am a sacred Tree of Life. My mind~body~spirit grows in Divine Light.
Please add an affirmative thought to continue your flow of positive energy
I....._____

CHAPTER 2

The Laws of the Universe

I have been repeatedly shown and understood for a long time, that there is greater meaning in every experience. I have lived it with trepidation and with joy. And because of that innate meaning, even when not yet visible, Divine Order and Divine Timing bless us with significant comprehension of the events in our lives. Hand and hand, one with our Higher Self, we are guided forward as the spiritual and physical truths reveal their deeper message and the path before us.

Divine Order, Divine Timing

~ To everything there is a season, and a time for every purpose under heaven ~
Ecclesiastes 3:1

The universe is governed by guiding principles, repeating and perpetual patterns that are visible in all aspects of life. Many of these principles are cyclical: the hours in a day, the phases of the moon, the cycles of seasons, and the growth of the human body. In addition there are spiritual laws, truths that are constant in all circumstances. They have existed in all of time, in all eternity.

It behooves us to be aware of these principles and their guidance as they assist us in being in alignment with soul energy. The consistency they represent in the physical world and the equilibrium they represent in the spiritual world are reliable references. Know then, that as you progress forward in your life, there are messages in the circumstances that surround you.

Divine Order and Divine Timing rest on the principle of connectedness, the relationship of one entity to another. These concepts parallel the Spiritual Laws in their instruction and insight, each association having specific relational purposes we are meant to learn from. Our actions create bidirectional intention. Energy projects outward into the universe and all those we interact with, while outcomes of that energy return to us. It is our heartfelt desire to be in a state of balance and the universe guides us to maintain that balance and alignment with source energy.

Living your life means walking the path of enlightenment. Walking forward, Divine Order and Divine Timing reveal information that guides you in a direction of service to your highest good and the highest good of all. Observing and listening are two key components to understanding these principles and your progress. In living your life you may experience episodes of frustration and even anger when what you believe should happen does not, even when things appear to be ready and complete. Remember that we are living our earthly life for purposes beyond

ourselves; to assist others on their journey and to assist in creating changes that are optimal for us to live in with unity and love.

~ The events in our lives happen in a sequence in time, but in their significance to ourselves they find their own order, with patience and quiet observation, these events will provide the seeker in you with a continuous thread of revelation ~
Eudora Welty
Novelist and photographer

Dependency is a relationship of power. When something is dependent, the more powerful factor must come first and the reliant factor cannot exist unless it is present. Through episodes of dependency we are able to gain confidence and become more independent selves. In our childhood we are *born dependent* to survive and must accomplish stages of growth to gain independence. *Independence* is an increasing aspect of our physical and psychological maturity and expanded authentic self.

Sequencing is a relationship of order. To proceed, to move forward, factors must align one after the other. There are many complex sequencing patterns in our lives that exist to assist us in navigating paths and obstacles. Sequencing patterns repeat in similar situations to promote our understanding and to help us embody learnings into our consciousness. When we are able to see sequencing patterns for the positive or negative effect they have on our lives, we can make decisions and choices from a higher perspective of awareness. Often relationship and career patterns are sequencing patterns.

Adjacency is a relationship of position relative to your position. The relationship may be temporary or permanent, obvious, or intuitive. Adjacency factors convey information about a person, place, or thing [relative to a moment in time] and serve to guide you to promote your safety, health, and growth.

Synchronicity is a relationship of meaningful events without an evident connection. Seemingly unrelated, these presumed coincidences provide an association one to the next that prompt further action. They are Divine Guidance in an energetic form and exist in our lives as instructional messages for us to act upon. Synchronicity realization requires mindful openness to consider factors beyond our understanding and to respond intuitively following our inner guidance.

Divine Timing is a relationship of alignment with Divine Order. When things align in particular order they are able to be activated. Like a catalyst, Divine Timing is the trigger that stimulates the progression of all things.

~ Things come suitable to their time ~
Enid Bagnold
British author and playwright

Divine Order and Divine Timing principles give us perspective into the meaning of situations, relationships and outcomes. When we observe from an elevated place of awareness and faith, we are being guided to the best possible outcomes for the highest good of all.

Discovery Thought....

Think about your current situation in life. What universal rules are guiding you? What do you believe you need to be aware of to make positive changes in your life ?

_____
_____
_____
_____
_____
_____
_____
_____
_____
_____
_____

Divine Timing asks you for patience and wisdom knowing that things are activated in alignment with Divine Order. What situations in your life are poised for Diving Timing to initiate action?

_____
_____
_____
_____
_____
_____
_____
_____
_____
_____
_____
_____
_____

Affirmation: My life is spiritually orchestrated by Divine Order and Divine Timing.
I trust in the wisdom of the Universe.
Please add an affirmative thought to continue your flow of positive energy
_I....._____

"I feel the presence of a higher power. I believe that what you give is what you get. It is universal law. I believe in the power of prayer and of words. I've learned that when you predict that negative things will happen, they do."
Alicia Keys
American singer, songwriter

Spiritual Laws

~ As long as one keeps searching, the answers come ~
Joan Baez
Folk singer, songwriter, activist

As we live our lives, make choices, and learn through experiences, it is important to remember that the Spiritual Laws of the Universe work in conjunction with Divine Order and Divine Timing.

When you encounter resistance in your life there are forces competing with source energy. Resistance is a message that asks for clarity. There is a push/pull feeling as the direction in which your mind or physical being is proceeding does not align with your spiritual guidance. Guidance always directs you in a positive way and asks you to pause, observe, and reflect.

~ And those who were seen dancing were thought to be insane
by those who could not hear the music ~
Friedrich Nietzsche
German philosopher, poet

As you explore your soul garden, the following spiritual laws are relevant to understanding and growth: seeds, stems, and flowers.

The Law of Divine Oneness states that everything in the Universe is interconnected. Every word, thought, belief, desire, decision, and action will have an impact on you and the world.

Connection is projected outward from you through energy vibrations. The results may or may not be immediately visible, but they have been initiated.

The Law of Attraction tells us that like attracts like. You attract what you project physically, verbally, behaviorally and vibrationally. This also applies to your thoughts and manifestations as you create what you focus on. Additionally, you attract what you are in the world.

The Law of Inspired Action instructs us that to live life fully we must actively pursue our goals. This includes thoughtfully visualizing what you desire and taking inspired, dedicated steps towards them. Each step, no matter how small, moves you in a direction closer to your purpose. All movement allows you to reassess, realign, and change course as needed.

The Law of Cause and Effect explains that all actions have a corresponding reaction. This law is reproduceable in science, math, physics, and by what we attract into our lives. Positive creates positive, negative creates negative. In the spiritual world the corresponding reaction is answer to prayer.

The Law of Compensation promises that you will receive what you give out. Compensation, or the return on your energy "investment" comes in many forms. Faith ensures us that all situations occur in the highest good of all. If we move forward in trust, putting forth our best effort, we will be rewarded with what is intended.

The Law of Polarity tells us that everything has an opposite and the very existence of these opposites allows us to better understand our life. Our goal is to exist in center balance, the core balance within us. By centering we can live in harmony, stabilizing the forces that pull us in one direction or another; between the light and the dark, the positive and negative, the truth and illusion. We are connected with this polarity to observe, experience, and become more of the person we are meant to be.

~ *Each place along the way is somewhere you had to be in order to be here* ~
Dr. Wayne Dyer
Self-help, spiritual author

Spiritual Laws abound in our lives. Every thought and action projects out into the world and initiates a response from others and the universe. We are empowered by these Laws to utilize them consciously and effectively to create abundance, Love and Light in the world.

Discovery Thought....
Reflect on your life path, the path you walk. What spiritual laws are evident in the outcomes you have experienced? How have these created prosperity in your life?

_____

_____

_____

_____

_____

_____

_____

_____

_____

_____

_____

_____

_____

_____

_____

_____

_____

Spiritual Laws continuously guide us. Which Laws do you consciously incorporate into your daily processes and practices?

_____
_____
_____
_____
_____
_____
_____
_____
_____
_____
_____
_____
_____
_____
_____
_____
_____

Affirmation: I embrace spiritual guidance. I ask for what I desire.
I receive what I project into the Universe.
Please add an affirmative thought to continue your flow of positive energy
I….._____

CHAPTER 3

The Human Experience

Birth, Our Emergence

Life on earth brings forth opportunity. It is the life we chose and the life we search for in the same moment. In return we are asked to pursue our highest good for the highest good of all.

See your life reflected in a deep pool of water that mirrors the heavens above you. Your face appears again and again within images of sky, and it within you, until all eternity projects into the pool; the last minutest image, which is the seed, the life incarnate.

~The true joy of life is not in the grand gesture but in the consecration of the moment~
Kent Nerburn
Author

Human experience begins with creation and continuously evolves as a journey of awakening. In her book *Simple Abundance*, Sarah Ban Breathnach tells us ... "Remember, before anything exists on earth, it exists fully formed in spirit. The Great Creator does not play favorites; each of us came into being to carry on the re-creation of the world through our gifts."

The word "reincarnation" expresses the philosophical or spiritual concept of our soul's rebirth. In Hinduism and Buddhism, reincarnation was believed to be a passage of enlightenment, and both Socrates and Plato included this philosophy in their teachings. Tribes of North American Indians including the Zuni and Mohave, believe that reincarnation also includes the ability of the soul to emerge in other life forms such as animals and birds.

Spiritually, reincarnation represents our conscious choice to purposefully be of service on earth to create and bring forth enlightenment. Your soul is *you*, and therefore reincarnates the true essence of who you are. With each lifetime we have opportunity to experience illumination, ascending levels of understanding, and expansion associated with our soul's purpose.

The subconscious mind is the aspect of the soul that stores memories and events as karma. Karma is the internal imprint of feelings, emotions, and perceptions. Within the subconscious these encounters build a library of interpretational references from which we draw upon in future time. Karma serves as an inner compass alerting us to situations and decisions that are important for growth. In the evolution of our lifetimes we are gifted with recurring processes by which we can reconcile karmic remnants (the imbalance within), to live authentically in peace and harmony.

We think of the ethereal as a heaven with all the human associated images. The puffy white clouds with cherubim and seraphim. Archangels with massive spreading wings and harps of gold. A majestic place of peace with pearly gates and a god on a throne. Sound familiar?

But what if the ethereal was another dimension of spiritual energy somewhere within the vapors of the atmosphere. And within this ethos of existence you were pure energy as well, the energy of your soul. What if your purpose in being this energy was to create... all things imaginable; goodness, love, abundance, peace. And every now and then.... your soul energy chose to be recreated again in physical form. Would you not be bringing heaven to earth?

In the process of bringing heaven to earth there are three phases of life in each creation; the Ethereal, the Physical/Spiritual, and the Transitional.

> ~ *How we remember, and what we remember, and why we remember*
> *form the most personal map of our individuality* ~
> Christina Baldwin
> Author, teacher

In the *Ethereal...*

We choose life purpose and our soul emerges past the veil, to be physically alive on the earth. Most often we do not remember the ethereal plane. The veil closes in an amnesiac episode to allow us to be fully present as a human being, to engage in all aspects of human life with all life forms. We are given opportunity to rediscover our authentic self as we evolve and aspire to be one with spirit.

> ~ *You don't have a soul.... You are a soul. You have a body, temporarily* ~
> Walter M. Miller Jr.
> American science fiction writer

In the Physical/Spiritual...

In this phase of our life the world inside of us becomes a dynamic network of vibrational communication and interpretation, channeling thoughts and messages. Energy flows to us and through us which we utilize to grow, experience, and further develop. We expand in many dimensions, always trying to create a world we wish to live in. Conscious thoughts become our reality. Our connection with spirit becomes our life line.

We develop, experience, and expand as a *physical, mindful, spiritual being.*

Our bodies are holy vessels that house our souls so we may live on the earthly plain. The body requires nourishment, respect, healing and activities which promote its optimal functioning. We are the stewards, the caretakers, responsible for its care.

Dr Wayne Dyer in his book *You Are What You Think*, gives us valuable insight in writing... "You would never abuse something that you thought was valuable.... Well, the same thing is true of yourself. If you think of yourself as valuable, very important, very significant as a human being, then you would never, ever abuse yourself, and you wouldn't allow someone else to abuse you. Most abuse that people endure... comes from a belief, a fundamental belief, that *what I am abusing isn't worth anything."*

Our body and mind are our connections with the physical world, while our spirit connects us to the Ethereal/the Universe. We go through our sacred heart to spirit and to access our soul garden.

~ *The opposite of life is not death. The opposite of death is birth.*
Life has no opposite ~
Eckhart Tolle
Spiritual teacher and author

In the Transitional...

When the human body can no longer support our biological needs it weakens and physically experiences death. Death is the final transition in an episode of one human lifetime, while our soul ascends to incorporate again into the Ethereal.

Transition is a passage of change. Each human life experiences many transitions in each life on earth. Transitions bridge episodes of learnings with levels of maturity, allowing us to evolve again. In transitioning we have opportunity to release that which no longer serves us: emotions, choices, regrets, sadness. In transitioning we become free to engage in new beginnings. We are able to create through recreation who we desire to be.

The three phases of life, the Ethereal, the Physical/Spiritual, and the Transitional, are continuing passageways for us to enter new dimensions of a spiritual being in human form. Possibilities are endless. We create our own reality and therefore the journey.

Discovery Thought...

What are your earliest recollections of your childhood? What emotions do you associate with them?

_____

_____

_____

_____

_____

_____

_____

_____

_____

_____

_____

_____

_____

As you live your life, give thanks and gratitude for your sacred vessel that houses your soul. How do you care for your body to promote its physical [body/mind] wellbeing?

_____
_____
_____
_____
_____
_____
_____
_____
_____
_____
_____
_____
_____
_____
_____
_____

Affirmation: I am the incarnation of my Highest Self.
I reflect my wholeness in all stages of growth.
Please add an affirmative thought to continue your flow of positive energy
I....._____

> ~ *There is an Indian proverb or axiom that says everyone is a house with*
> *four rooms; a physical, a mental, an emotional, and a spiritual* ~
> Rumor Godden
> British author

Spiritual Life Within the Vessel

There are three integrated forms of life energy within our human vessel: the Mind, the Body and the Spirit.

The Body *is a temple*, a holy place that is made in the image of our creator. It is a miraculous work of art, structure, and function that nourishes our physical being and mind. The human body is a universe unto itself, wherein every organ, vessel, muscle, nerve, tissue, bone, and cell has specific capabilities and purpose.

Before we were born we were designed. Conception begins a series of miraculous processes as unique strands of infinitesimal DNA weave complex codes, the blueprints to build our structure, gender, and interconnectedness. Everything symmetrical, balanced and woven by Divine Plan. There is nothing by chance.

In our earliest form, the embryo follows specific stages of formation, yet each of us is a unique individual. Each phase of our development enhances growth so we can functionally utilize all capabilities we are blessed with. Within the body there are specific elements that act as messengers and receivers to initiate responses that promote optimum health and physiological balance.

> ~ *The body is a sacred garment. It's your first and last garment; it is what you enter*
> *life in and what you depart life with, and it should be treated with honor* ~
> Martha Graham
> American modern dancer and choreographer

The Mind is credited with being our primary source of intelligence. Through thinking, reasoning, and understanding we determine our thoughts, behaviors, and actions. The *Brain* is an organ of the body, dense tissue and matter, which conducts and transmits signals to stimulate actions. The *Mind* is the culmination of that connectedness, interpreting and instructing our body actively and passively, voluntarily and involuntarily to optimize its collective reasoning.

Thoughts are processes of energy transmission. Using the mind we create ideas, feelings, and responses. We choose to envelope them, ignore them, or project them. Regardless of their source, thoughts give insight to our personality, life situations, and our interpretation of states of happiness, challenge, emotion, and fear.

Emotions are the products of sensory perception. Sensory receptors transmit signals through our body to be interpreted by the mind. Emotions are powerful stimulators of feelings. Feelings embed impressions that influence the way in which we react to sensory stimuli now and in the future.

Emotions are often described as another dimension of self, an additional layer to mind~body~spirit. Different from physical characteristics of our being, emotions begin to bridge vibrational frequencies from mind to heart, the entry to spirit. It is through emotion that we embody the physical and mindful aspects of the world and discover the meaning they hold for our lives. Emotions frequently override logic and objectivity. The release of past emotional patterns is essential in becoming an enlarged self, the self we are meant to be.

In order to understand emotions we need to center ourselves. When a wave of emotion rises from within, accept it as being genuine and allow it to process. What you feel is what you interpret. What you feel is what you know. Center your mind~body~spirit within your heart. Begin conscious breathing to release energy and open passageways for new thought to come forward. Visualize your heart space and its expansiveness. Embrace yourself with your loving arms, encircling the *ALL* of you. You are loved. You are safe...... you are given the time you need to process all that comes forward. When you experience new peace and balance you are ready to move on. Trust the guidance inside you to be the person you desire to be.

The mind stores memory and knowledge and is an important source of learning by converting experiences into a perceived reality. These perceptions and inferences guide choices, communications, behaviors, and actions. In the earthly plane we use our minds as a navigational tool to effectively manage the physical self.

Beyond ourselves, we can open our minds to receive guidance and messages from the flow of Divine Energy channeled to us. When we accept this limitless gift the universe is able to assist us in envisioning and creating that which we desire.

~ The shell must break before the bird can fly ~
Alfred Lloyd Tennyson
British Poet

<u>*The Spirit*</u> *is one with our higher self,* our being of Light and Love within us, connecting our body and mind to greater awareness and purpose. Through our heart space we are able to connect with spirit and be in a place of oneness with soul, the life force energy that guides our journey and reveals all that is, all that has been, and all that will be. When we are with spirit we are in unity with the whole, one as infinite one.

There are things we believe and things we know. The understanding, attachment, and power we give each word, believing and knowing, creates commitments and expectations of ourselves and others.

I Believe ..... is an act of the mind. It conveys a level of confidence upon the subject and as a result there is a level of faith that is generated. There is an expectation that something will come forward, something in return.

I Know... is an act of the spirit. To know is an embodiment of truth without doubt or distance. Knowing is finding your inner truth.... it has been trying to find you all your lifetimes.

There are no expectations with knowing beyond its own truth.

~ Earth is crammed with heaven ~
Elizabeth Barrett Browning
British poet

Spiritual life within the vessel integrates mind~body~spirit into one unifying form. As an integrated being we are capable of discovering and knowing our truths and purpose.

Discovery Thoughts....
Emotions create feelings that are processed through the mind. How do emotions effect your response to life events?

_____

_____

_____

_____

_____
_____
_____
_____
_____
_____
_____
_____
_____

What are things you believe in, have faith in? What do you expect in return for those beliefs?

_____
_____
_____
_____
_____
_____
_____
_____
_____
_____
_____
_____
_____
_____
_____
_____
_____

Affirmation: I live in truth.
My spirit guides me to express my integrity and authenticity.
Please add an affirmative thought to continue your flow of positive energy.
*I…..*_____

To love oneself is the beginning of a lifelong romance."
Oscar Wilde
Irish poet and playwright

Dimensions of Mind~Body~Spirit

~ Seek not outside yourself, heaven is within ~
Mary Lou Cook
Actress, singer, dancer

The dimensions of the human self are vast. Each level adds depth to our ability to process and comprehend information and respond in our best interest.

Developmental stages are not limited to age. Stages are reflective of our growth in living, with each level having intended learnings. Depending upon how each level is accomplished, we acquire abilities and understandings.

~ We cannot teach people anything; we can only help them discover it within themselves ~
Galileo Galilei
Italian astronomer, physicist, engineer

The Body is primarily a nurturing and sensing vehicle for our growth and maintenance.

The Mind is a complex communicator that receives information, interprets it, relays it, and stores it.

The Spirit is an energy receptor and transmitter, a source of enlightenment.

Our mind~body~spirit is blessed with the capacity to communicate. Communication is our gift to ourselves and to the world. As functional beings of Divine Light we are operational on three planes: the self (communication), the self with others (connection), and beyond the self (extension).

Communication [with Self]

~ In your silence, God's silence ceases ~
Paramahansa Yogananda
Indian monk, yogi, and guru

The mind is a vibrant wellspring of information, ideas, and thoughts waiting to be processed and conveyed. We communicate verbally, behaviorally, and creatively within ourselves and to others. What we communicate resonates within us and around us. Our words express desires, needs, and feelings that create the environment we live in, the "environmental soil" we plant seeds in. Communicating fully and effectively is essential to experience balance, harmony, and growth.

There are numerous ways that the mind~body~spirit communicates with us, with Self. Communication is necessary to guide and facilitate choices. Communication with the self builds personality, self-esteem, self-worth and character; what we believe about ourselves.

These beliefs are powerful impressions upon the mind and are fastidious in their hold upon our psyche.

The ego is a psychological dimension of the mind. Memory storage and instinctual frameworks [what you are prone to do] reside in the unconscious, while personality uncovers itself in the conscious mind. Personality, the self we outwardly display and self-esteem, the internal value we give ourselves, are powerful influencers in decisions and growth. Like chains that secure us in a stationary pose, ego beliefs continuously feed themselves on what we attract and absorb, always resurrecting feelings of insecurity and fear to remain in power.

~ Nothing can cure the soul but the senses,
just as nothing can cure the senses but the soul ~
Oscar Wilde
Irish poet and playwright

Senses – Senses begin to develop as part of the fetal growth process. Scientists have well documented the fetus's response to various stimuli: music, massage/caresses and familiar voices.

Our senses serve to aid us in perceiving and interpreting. Physical senses leave impressions, the physical connecting with the mind. These include sight, smell, hearing, taste, and touch.

The sixth sense, intuition, is a spiritual to mind communication, an inner guidance, that allows us to communicate with what is invisible in the physical world.

Free Will – Free will is a state of balance that allows us to do, say, and think without constraints. When we exercise free will we invoke personal power.

Instinct – Instinct is the ability to assess surrounding stimuli and respond without further reasoning. When we instinctually know something our conscious and subconscious mind trigger an inherent response.

Choice – Choice is our ability to implement decisions that promote further action. Personal freedom is making choices and acting [consciously] in our best interest. Personal freedom choices are not influenced by fear, anger, pride or emotions.

Emotions – Emotions are expressed in feelings that arise from sensory dimensions within our fields of awareness and perception. We choose how to process emotions with responses ranging from superficial to visceral. Emotions allow us to embody an experience and retain it as an impression upon the conscious and subconscious mind. Communicating and understanding our emotions is a process of growth and maturity that promotes healing.

Self-Worth / Self-Esteem – In early child hood we begin to develop self-worth and self-esteem. Although they are similar and increase self-confidence, they are different in how we process them. Self-esteem is a form of respect. It is the appreciation of the abilities we have acquired and display. Self-worth is the measured value we give ourselves based on our expectations and achievement of goals.

Influenced and reinforced by external factors, we begin to judge our appearance, actions and beliefs as good or bad, positive or negative. We wrestle internally with the need to be loved and accepted by others versus our own thoughts and free will. What we believe about ourselves dictates internal communication and abilities to optimally grow and develop. With further growth and understanding of truth and authenticity, self-worth and self-esteem become a connection of the Higher Self.

The Inner Child - The Inner Child is the essence of early childhood, the original true self, pure and genuine before the influences of family, society, and ego. The inner child lives in the subconscious mind and beckons you to reawaken the playful, innocent, adventurous younger self within you.

Chakra Energy – Chakra energy flows from the cosmos to the crown chakra (top of the head) when we open to its flow. Its vibrational energy continues to move through us connecting the seven main power chakra centers within our body. Chakra energy balances our body and mind to integrate healing and to open ourselves to enlightenment. Through the 4th Chakra, the heart chakra, we are connected to our Higher Self and Soul.

Dreams – Images, thoughts, and stories come to us in dreams, in our subconscious sleep state, and impart a deeper meaning to our lives. Dreams are visions meant to guide us to present, past and future.

> ~ *I've dreamt in my life dreams that have stayed with me ever after, and changed my ideas.*
> *They've gone through and through me, like wine through water, and altered the color of my mind* ~
> Emily Bronte
> British novelist and poet

Connection [from Self]

We are innately social beings. We build relationships, families, groups and communities in order to relate to one another. We desire to share and receive, develop and create, and experience a broader knowing of ourselves by knowing another person.

> ~ *Kind hearts are the gardens.*
> *Kind thoughts are the roots.*
> *Kind words are the blossoms.*
> *Kind deeds are the fruits* ~
> Kirpal Singh
> Spiritual master

From our Body we can behave, act and physically demonstrate in ways that project our communication energy out into the world. Expressions, mannerisms, physical connection,

avoidance, and aggressiveness display our intent. We can display openness in allowing the flow of communication to move outward and then return, or model body language which blocks its circulation. Our body communicates as an invitation or a barrier.

From our Mind we can think and verbalize what we believe and desire. We express in a positive or negative manner. Through thoughts and words we manifest content and create affirmative steps aligning us with intended outcomes.

Communication is a vehicle transporting the products of the mind to connect with the universe and with others. How we communicate and what we communicate is interpreted and generates a response. The response may or may not be directed back to us.

Communication can be silent as in the act of conscious listening. Although we may hear others, conscious listening is an attentive process of focus, connecting with their message.

Listening allows others to share and release their opinions and needs and allows us to gain insight into their world and daily life. Conscious listening evokes compassion and builds relationships.

From our Spirit we connect with our higher self and the spiritual universe through prayer, meditation and expansion. Spirit guides us to multidimensional awareness of our self and soul purpose. Spiritual communication is an unveiling of the truth we are open to receiving. As in all relationships, frequent honest connection with our spiritual self is key to its evolution and expansion.

Extension [beyond Self]

~ *I am rooted, but I flow* ~
Virginia Woolf
British modernist writer

We have capabilities to transmit and receive energy beyond the traditional three dimensional world. These transmissions can be through body, mind or spirit to other people, living things, energy centers, past lives and those in the angelic and ethereal realm.

The universe and spirit continuously transmit energy in the form of guidance and messages.

It may be expressed as a "nagging voice inside" or the thought that "just won't go away". With growth and openness we learn how to listen, hear, and interpret.

A *clairsentient* is a person who has the ability to sense the energy of a location, a person, or an object, whereas a *clairaudient* is able to hear internal or external vibrational messages. A *claircognizant* receives and interprets information through intrinsic knowledge as it flows to their mind including information about the future.

Telepathy is a form of extrasensory perception (ESP), an ability to transfer and/or receive thoughts through means other than the five physical senses. Telepathy may be referred to as channeled or clairvoyant.

Transmission is the ability to silently message thought and energy for the purpose of enhancing life. Reiki is an example of transmission where positive energy flows from the hands of the practitioner to the client's body to promote balance and wellness.

Transcendence is an existence or experience of consciousness beyond the normal or physical level, beyond the limitations we associate with a physical realty. People who have described an "outer body occurrence" have experienced transcendence.

Ascension is a process by which we achieve higher dimensional understanding and function. It involves awakening, purifying, releasing, rebirth and ascension, through which we become one in unity with Divine Life. Ascension processes occur throughout our lifetime and do not require physical death.

Using these dimensional models and guideposts, think of how you have experienced greater connection. Think of your journey as a never ending life process and know that what you aspire to be and do is within your capabilities. It is all only a thought away.

~ From the beginning I had a sense of destiny, as though my life was assigned to me by fate and had to be fulfilled. This gave me an inner security, and though I could never prove it to myself it proved itself to me. I did not have this certainty, it had me ~
Carl Jung
Swiss psychiatrist and psychoanalyst

We have multiple ways within ourselves of interpreting and processing energy communication and extensive ways of extending ourselves beyond our physical being.

Our abilities to communicate are on three levels; with Self, from Self, and beyond Self, and depend upon our capabilities and surrounding environment. The powers of energy communication and transmission allow us to expand in all dimensions of mind~body~spirit. We are whole in our self-discovery when we are open to explore all that exists in the world around us and within us.

Discovery Thoughts....

Communication with Self is very personal. How does your internal communication promote your growth?

_____

_____

_____

_____

_____

_____

_____

_____

_____

_____

_____

_____

_____

_____

All relationships are built upon communications from self, and reflect the wholeness of mind~body~spirit. How honestly and openly do you feel you communicate with others?

_____

_____

_____

_____

_____

_____

_____

_____

_____

_____

_____

_____

_____

_____

How have you experienced communication beyond yourself? What do you believe is its purpose? How did you respond?

_____
_____
_____
_____
_____
_____
_____
_____
_____
_____
_____
_____
_____
_____
_____

Affirmation: I embrace my self-discovery. Communication leads me to expansion.
Please add an affirmative thought to continue your flow of positive energy
*I.....*_____

CHAPTER 4

One With Spirit

Growth occurs in all phases of our lives and in all dimensions. It is limitless. If we try to quantify and measure it, we are focusing on physical aspects that the ego mind uses to compare us with all things. Continuing to move forward in trust, exploring that which is before us, we walk our soul path with Higher Self.

> ~ *Our birth is but a sleep and a forgetting:*
> *The soul that rises, with us, our life's star, Hath had elsewhere its setting, and cometh from afar:*
> *Not in entire forgetfulness...* ~
> William Wordsworth
> English romantic poet

In the garden, we are one with spirit in energy form. The soul garden *IS* a Garden of Eden, created by us as a unique, beautiful reflection of the eternity of our soul.

As Divine Beings we create a sanctuary that speaks to us as an individual. We desire to create a refuge, a space where the burdens of the physical world will not constrain us, nor limit us in fully experiencing the universal world we live in. The Soul Garden is a state of endless freedom and enlightenment.

The Higher Self

> ~ *I learned that the real creator was my inner self, the Shakti .....*
> *That desire to do something is God inside talking through us* ~
> Michele Shea
> Author

The Higher Self is the connection of our Spirit to our physical being and soul. It is an aspect of ourselves that unites our energy and understanding in the earthly world with the spiritual world. The Higher Self is our most authentic and elevated form of consciousness. Unlike the Tree of Life, our higher self is not influenced by karma. It speaks in truth and wisdom in the present from connection with the Divine and the universe.

The Higher Self knows where you have been, where you are and where you are meant to be. It knows the choices you have made and the paths you have walked. It is always in balance and alignment with soul energy, guiding you to a state of wellbeing and eternal love. The Higher Self seeks to show you the answers to the questions that are always within you.

Dimensions of Oneness...

~ Your capacity to be fully present expands dramatically when you stop identifying yourself as a time bound human being separate from others, and start experiencing life as a timeless spiritual being at one with all creation ~
Phil Bolsta
Author, spiritual guide

The following are dimensions of our oneness with spirit which become embodied in the garden. Once experienced, we are able to bring them into the earthly plane through spirit's connection with Higher Self and then to our mind. The level with which your physical being is able to recreate dimensions of oneness is proportional to the consistency of living in Divine Light and Love.

Serenity – A State of Being

~ Everything has its wonders, even darkness and silence, and I learn whatever state I may be in, therein to be content ~
Helen Keller
American author, activist

You are your Soul Garden. You are the life that plants seeds, nourishes growth, and blooms in spiritual presence. Your garden reflects what has been, is now, and what will be. As a gardener of your sacred soil, you are the guardian for its wellbeing and that which it brings forth. Your garden exists as you exist. Your garden thrives as you thrive. Your garden replicates the Light and Love you bring into the world.

Serenity is a state of being. When you are in the garden, observe the beauty which surrounds you and breathe in the purity and freshness of life. The garden abounds with your growth. Bless your family for their relationship gifts to you. Be thankful for life's experiences, the people and events that have assisted you in becoming who you are. Express gratitude for those who give of themselves each day to bring food to your table, shelter to your body, and love into your life. Know that you are only who you are as a result of them, and as a result of all things you connect with.

Stress is a sensation we embody in response to circumstances we feel are overwhelming. Its effects can range from despair to anger, from vulnerability to determination. Over time stress creates issues with health and wellness. At its basis, stress is akin to fear of losing control as we strive and struggle to maintain superiority above the circumstances we live with.

Stress misleads us by illusion to believe that if we were just *MORE* than what we are we could master the current circumstances. Ego rules our desire for control and all aspects of being *MORE*.

In the garden, everything exists as we have created it. The garden is not effected by the external circumstances that impact us in the physical world.

As a state of being, serenity creates wholeness by promoting peace in our life and in our mind.

Serenity unifies equilibrium with tranquility in all living things, with source energy and our soul's purpose. In this place of high frequency energy you are in harmony with your own truth.

Discovery Thoughts...

Picture yourself sitting in your soul garden under The Tree of Life, observing all you have created. What do you see that brings you a feeling of serenity?

_____
_____
_____
_____
_____
_____
_____
_____
_____
_____
_____
_____
_____
_____
_____

How do you manage stressful situations that occur in your life? Is there something that creates stress in your life you would like to release the need for control over?

_____
_____
_____
_____
_____
_____
_____
_____
_____
_____
_____
_____
_____
_____
_____

Affirmation: I am the serenity of my garden. I bring peace to my life and into the world.
Please add an affirmative thought to continue your flow of positive energy
I....._____

"Spirituality is not a formula; it is not a test. It is a relationship. Spirituality is not about competency; it is about intimacy. Spirituality is not about perfection, it is about connection."
Mike Yaconelli
Writer, theologian

Alignment – A State of Balance

> ~ *Learn to get in touch with the silence within yourself*
> *and know that everything in this life has a purpose* ~
> Elizabeth Kubler-Ross
> Swiss-American psychiatrist and author

We are continually adjusting to achieve symmetry and stability with the energy that encircles us. This energy comes from people, situations, work, responsibilities, challenges, and events occurring in our lives and on the earth. You are at the center of your vortex with life's concentric rings circling outside of your energetic space. You choose what to absorb and what to allow to be its own entity. Your balance is internal and not reliant on other energy or energy state to be whole.

Being in balance is a process of active movement as energy flows to and from you. You are not stationary, nor do you maintain it by staying fixed in one position. Like a boat on the ocean, energy comes in waves; the boat adjusts by leaning one way and then the other to remain upright, to retain its equilibrium. Acts of balance are horizontal processes that integrate with energy coming to you. This horizontal balance then supports the vertical connection of your internal energy with Higher Self.

To align is a unification, your Higher Self with your balanced being. Defined as "the quality of forming a pleasing and consistent whole", when you align you are detaching from your personal self, the ego self, to create a higher level of vibrational frequency within you.

To be whole with Higher Self and the Universe is an upward alignment within you and from you. The Law of Attraction reminds us that we attract what we think, say and do, like a magnet pulling life force energy within.

> ~*The interior life is merely what is not exterior*~
> Thomas Merton
> Spiritual author, activist and Trappist monk

Being mindful of decisions and actions promotes our abilities to remain in balance and alignment. Listening, observing, detaching .... all require conscious awareness. Know that everything we do is opportunity to honor ourselves, and that by doing so, we honor others.

Discovery Thoughts...

What practices and processes do you use to maintain balance in your life?

_____

_____

_____

_____

_____

_____
_____
_____
_____
_____
_____

How do you center yourself and align with Higher Self?

_____
_____
_____
_____
_____
_____
_____
_____
_____
_____
_____
_____
_____
_____

Affirmation: I am balanced and centered. I align with soul energy.
Please add an affirmative thought to continue your flow of positive energy
*I....*_____

Flow - A State of Allowing

> ∼ *To the ego mind, surrender means giving up.*
> *To the spiritual mind, surrender means giving in and receiving* ∼
> Marianne Williamson
> American author and spiritual leader

Allowing is a state of surrender, yielding to the flow of Divine Energy to direct and guide you. When we believe in the universal flow of good, we are able to release fears and believe that all situations are intended for their highest good.

With grace we gain the capacity to transcend matters transpiring at the personal level and see beyond the illusion of circumstances and emotions to a deeper truth.

We *Open... Allow... Accept... Receive...*

We *Open our minds.... Allow spirit to come forward.... Accept intrinsic goodness... and Receive it into our heart.*

Resistance is felt as a messenger signifying that actions are moving us forward. We gain traction with resistance to create time and space for us to reexamine our purpose and remain open to the flow of energy. Resistance heralds progress and a time to reassess, realign, and gather strength.

Flow also allows us to confer energy upon something with conscious thought and positive intention. In manifestation we are conferring mindful energy upon a thought to magnify it into form. When we bless something we are conferring spiritual energy upon it, setting an intention in the highest good.

> ∼ *Everything in life that we really accept undergoes a change.*
> *So suffering must become love. That is the mystery* ∼
> Katherine Mansfield
> Short story writer and poet

To be present and become one with the flow of energy, of life, we must Open.... Allow.... Accept... and Receive; being present to the evolving wisdom and guidance that is contained within.

Discovery Thoughts....

Fears may prevent us from surrendering to the flow of Divine Energy. How do you open yourself to accept and receive the flow of this intrinsic goodness?

_____
_____
_____
_____
_____
_____
_____
_____
_____
_____
_____
_____

Affirmation: I Open... Allow... Accept... Receive...
I am expansive in the flow of Divine Energy.
Please add an affirmative thought to continue your flow of positive energy
I...._____

Faith – A State of Belief

~ You are not living by human laws but by divine laws.
Expect miracles and see them take place.
Hold ever before you the thought of prosperity and abundance,
and know that doing so sets in motion forces that will bring it into being ~
Eileen Caddy
Spiritual teacher and a founder of the Findhorn foundation

Faith opens us to optimism and hope. To see beyond where we are to what we believe will be better; a situation, a relationship, a place. Hope strengthens conviction.

With faith we activate intentions and believe all things are possible. We expect there will be positive changes in answer to our requests and prayers.

In her book *The Gifts of Imperfection*, Brene Brown defines hope as a cognitive process, a way of thinking, and clarifies that hope is not an emotion. I would add that although *not an emotion*, hope evokes emotional connectiveness to what we believe will come forward.

~ Faith is the bird that feels the light when the dawn is still dark ~
Rabindranath Tagore
Bengali poet, writer and composer

Knowing that God exists in all situations, we are never alone or abandoned. The act of faith creates a bond that solidifies us with purpose and destination. With faith we believe in something greater than ourselves.

Discovery Thoughts....

Take a moment to consider your present life circumstances. In faith, what do you believe will come forward?

_____
_____
_____
_____
_____
_____
_____
_____
_____
_____
_____

Affirmation: I live in Faith. With faith I activate all intentions to their highest good.
Please add an affirmative thought to continue your flow of positive energy
*I.....*_____

Love – a State of Communion

> *∼ I have listened to the realm of the spirit.*
> *I have heard my own soul's voice, and I have remembered*
> *that love is the complete and unifying thread of existence ∼*
> Mary Casey
> Author

Love is a process of evolution, of unfolding, like the blossoms of a flower. Agape, or unconditional love, is the selfless expression of love outward without expectation of return.

The soul only knows and understands love. It will only grow love. Love of yourself. Love as a gift to others. Self-love, being accepting of yourself and the love of others towards you. To be able to love fully you must love yourself. This is a priority and necessity.

The fourth chakra energy center is located in our heart space and is the energy bridge between the physical self [body/mind] and the spiritual self. In her book, *Anatomy of the Spirit*, Caroline Myss describes the fourth chakra as "the central powerhouse of the human energy system. The middle chakra, it mediates between the body and spirit and determines their health and strength…. The chakra embodies the spiritual lesson that teaches us how to act out of love and compassion and recognize that the most powerful energy we have is love. Love is Divine Power."

Love exists in many forms …. compassion, kindness, communication, and touch. Touch is the physical connection of one being to another that can be given and received as an act of love. We begin to learn about love at tender ages, embedding these learnings in our hearts and minds. With these experiences the seeds of understanding self-love are sown. Feeling worthy and being valued allow us to trust and open ourselves to give and receive love, and accept God's love for us.

In the eyes of love we are all equal. In the eyes of love we are all one in unity. We must love ourselves in order to truly love others. We must embrace a sensitivity and kindness to understand our needs, and enable a strength and charity to accept and understand who we are. To care for yourself with love is an equally generous gesture that elevates your capacity to love all.

Love is also a healing force of energy. To feel another's circumstances and emotions is a benevolent gift of love that sends hope and healing into their lives. Love plants seeds.

> *∼ The most important thing in life is to learn how to give out love,*
> *and how to let it come in ∼*
> Morrie Schwartz
> Professor and author

Grace, the gift of benevolence, is God's unconditional love. Through spirit each of us is made in His image, unique and gifted. The love of our Creator exists irrespective of our love for Him. What we need we are able to receive. What we receive we are able to magnify. Grace blesses us to share, to embrace and release, to give for the benefit of human kind, nature and our earth.

~ Every act of love is a work of peace, no matter how small ~
Mother Teresa
Albanian-Indian Catholic nun and missionary

Love as communion, connects us to all people and all circumstances. By design, it is intended to be freely given to nurture, support and elevate ourselves and others.

Love is the greatest gift we have been blessed with.

Discovery Thoughts....

Picture yourself as the beautiful sacred being you are. How do you practice self-love?

_____

_____

_____

_____

_____

_____

_____

_____

_____

_____

_____

_____

_____

_____

_____

_____

Think about all the dimensions of love in your life. How have you experienced love as a healing force?

_____

_____

_____

_____

_____

_____

_____

_____

_____

_____

_____
_____
_____
_____
_____

Affirmation: My love is limitless. Grace blesses me with communion for all living things.
Please add an affirmative thought to continue your flow of positive energy
I....._____

Prayer – A State of Grace

> ~ *Prayer is not asking. It is a longing of the soul....*
> *In prayer it is better to have a heart without words than words without a heart* ~
> Mahatma Gandhi
> Indian lawyer, political activist, writer

Prayer is a heartfelt conversation with the Divine Creator, the force you believe exists above yourself and all others, that connects us spiritually to love and unity. We pray to connect, to give thanks, to ask, to share.... to know a God.

Prayer is talking to God. In meditation God is talking to us. Sometimes we ask, sometimes we listen and sometimes we give of ourselves by offering to be of service. In affirmation we are grateful for our gifts. In appreciation, we give thanks for things that are coming forward and for those already present. Prayer is faith in process.

When we commune with God we share from our hearts. We focus on God, not ourselves, and know that in His Divine wisdom and timing all is abundantly coming forward. We give thanks for all there is, and know that all that will be, is as well.

All thought is a form of prayer, a conversation through the mind to our Higher Self, spirit, and the Divine. In prayer we create reflection and connection that poses our questions and heartfelt desires. In the quietness of stilled heart space, we are supported in all ways. When we offer love and faith we receive blessings in bountiful ways we could never imagine.

All prayer is answered. Perhaps not always in the way we anticipate, but answered to support us and lead us onward. Joan Chittister in her monthly publication of *The Monastic Way,* tells us that "We do not pray in order to control God, We pray in order to become new within ourselves, to see differently, to see right.... Prayer simply opens us to God. After that, everything in life becomes the presence of God to us."

We become new with prayer as we are blessed with enlightenment. As you walk in the soul garden be present as an enlightened being. The Soul Garden is a place of reflection as much as growth. A place of continued prayer and thanksgiving.

*~The power in committing something to prayer comes not when I make
a request, but when I release my attachment to the outcome ~*
The Daily Word
Inspirational publication by Unity

In a state of grace, prayer becomes an act of love and thanksgiving. All thought is prayer connecting us with our Higher Self, with spirit, with our Divine Creator. Prayer enlightens us to be of service and live in union with all people and all things.

Discovery Thoughts.....
How do you choose to communicate with the Divine Creator?

_____
_____
_____
_____
_____
_____
_____
_____
_____
_____
_____
_____
_____

What prayers have been answered in your life? How have those experiences changed you?

_____
_____
_____
_____
_____
_____
_____
_____
_____
_____
_____
_____
_____

Affirmation: My life is a prayer of thanksgiving. Prayer enlightens me.
Please add an affirmative thought to continue your flow of positive energy.
*I.....*_____

Community - A State of Unity

> ~ *My lifetime listens to yours* ~
> Muriel Reikeyser
> American poet and political-social activist

Unity is wholeness beyond the self, one with all living things. It is a level of completeness which elevates us to a higher level of understanding, giving and receiving.

Forming relationships with others is our first experience with unity. Relationships reflect information back to us; who we are and where we are in our life processes. As we become more independent and self-aware our needs change, and thus the substance of our relationships change. Relationships build upon foundations. They are a continual pathway of exploration as we learn more about ourselves, our needs, and aspirations.

In the soul garden we see relationships reflected in the growth of plants. Some are blooming, some have wilted, and some are tender seedlings. All relationships assist us in growth and should be honored. When we are in union with life we recognize that even though we are each a unique individual we are all the same. We are Divine Beings of Light and Love.

> ~ *If you look deeply into the palm of your hand, you will see your parents and*
> *all generations of your ancestors. All of them are alive in this moment.*
> *Each is present in your body.*
> *You are the continuation of each of these people* ~
> Thich Nhat Hanh
> Vietnamese Buddhist monk and peace activist

We are meant to live in unity with all things. To share, to grow, to mature. Just as the plants in our garden, we are meant to support and enhance each other's purpose and life. Community is a process of sharing while continuing to integrate and develop.

Discovery Thoughts....

With increasing independence and self-awareness our needs change, and thus the substance of our relationships change. What do you value in a relationship?

_____

_____

_____

_____

_____

_____

_____

_____

_____

_____
_____
_____

Reflecting on your past relationships, who has influenced your growth the most?

_____
_____
_____
_____
_____
_____
_____
_____
_____
_____
_____
_____
_____
_____

How do you mentor others to support their growth and enlargement?

_____
_____
_____
_____
_____
_____
_____
_____
_____
_____
_____
_____
_____
_____
_____
_____

Affirmation: I bloom in stages of completeness.
My blossom supports the growth of others.
Please add an affirmative thought to continue your flow of positive energy.
*I.....*_____

CHAPTER 5

Life in the Garden

~ It was when she was all alone outside, in her yard, when the plants became her companions and their conversations flowed, when the sky played with her hair and the grass comforted her steps... when life no longer surrounded her, but became her - that was when she sat in the middle of god, and when god sat in the middle of her ~
Terri St. Cloud
Author and artist

From the Tree of Life, we create our soul garden. Energy, in the form of life force, creates seeds from thoughts and actions that germinate to become seedlings. Seedlings over time grow from roots into plants with stems, leaves, and blossoms. Each seedling vine and corresponding blossom are unique to an aspect of our life. We are always in the process of becoming. We are always growing upward in supplication, guided by light.

You have the ability to observe and reflect on your life processes and accumulated blossoms as you walk among them, appreciating your gifts and accomplishments. You become aware of life changes and choices that altered your direction. You become aware of further growth and authenticity which guided you back to alignment. It is all within your capability. Know that your garden is a place of discovery and wisdom.

The Helix of Growth – The Garden Matrix

~ Then I began to realize that I had to take another step in my evolution and growth ~
Eileen Caddy
Spiritual teacher and a founder of the Findhorn foundation

The Helix of Growth is an internal support to the stems of our plants, to the support of our spiritual being, and to the actionizing component of our development and maturation. Choices we make influence our growth, wellness, and consciousness as we interpret and embody their outcomes. Our ability to make choices corresponds to our capabilities, knowledge, independence, needs and aspirations. These change over time as we increasingly understand ourselves and our life purpose.

Within the stem of our plants, The Helix of Growth curls like DNA strands and continues to twist in repeated steps of advancement: Development, Experience, Expansion.

Leaves of Progression mark the incorporation of learning that occurs at each plateau of the helix. To begin growth, we set an intention – by affirmation, desire, or prayer.

The stem of the plant continues to develop into a bud and will yield a blossom when the plant has ripened to its fullest state of learning. Blossoms may occur singularly or in groups. They may be partially or fully opened. Blossoms indicate that an attribute towards wholeness has achieved a level of expansion.

~ That is what learning is.
You suddenly understand something you have understood all your life, but in a new way ~
Doris Lessing
British Zimbabwean novelist

Life in the Soul Garden is one of growth. Growth occurs with development, experience, and expansion. These are influenced by our choices and free will.

Discovery Thoughts...

Using the Helix of Growth as a model, what process aspect of your development, experience and expansion are you currently in?

_____

_____

_____

_____

_____

_____

_____

_____

_____

_____

_____

_____

_____

What do you feel are the next steps in evolving your life?

_____

_____

_____

_____

_____

_____

_____

_____

_____

_____

_____

_____

_____

Affirmation: I grow with the freedom of my choices.
My life continuously creates through expansion.
Please add an affirmative thought to continue your flow of positive energy.
*I.....*_____

"Growth is the only evidence of life."
John Henry Newman
English theologian and Catholic Cardinal

There are three *Steps to Advancement in Each Helix of Growth*:

> *~ Our most important decisions are discovered, not made ~*
> Anne Wilson Schaef
> Clinical psychologist and author

Development: With each stage of development we increase abilities. These can be physical, mental, or spiritual. Each stage allows us to grow our skills, insight, and competence.

Development increases confidence and the will to strive to be and do *more*.

Experience: All experiences are learnings. We experience consciously or subconsciously, actively or passively. In the process of experiencing we choose next actions and establish leaves of progression, the outcomes of our learnings.

Many things influence decision making. We may be guided from the Higher Self or affected by external stimuli. Ego imparts its messages to keep us bound to the physical self, aspiring to control, and put our needs above all other considerations. Feelings, perceptions, opinions, and judgments can emotionally cloud objectivity and reasoning.

Ultimately, it is not what we choose that matters. Our power to influence future outcomes lies in our **reasons** for making a certain choice. When our choices are in alignment with authenticity and higher self they are blessed.

Expansion: Expansion is the result of the embodiment of learnings. With expansion we grow in wisdom, understanding, intuition, and acceptance. Expansion allows us to view and approach the world with increased awareness, opening ourselves more fully to the flow of Divine Love and Light. Expansion is the progressive growth of trust.

> *~ When we come to an edge*
> *we come to a frontier that tells us that we are now about to become*
> *more than we have ever been before ~*
> William Irwin Thompson
> American social philosopher and poet

Growth is evolution in three phases: Development, Experience, and Expansion.

We gain abilities, insight, wisdom and confidence in each phase which encourages us to continue to do more and be more. Expansion blesses us with increasing trust in the Universe.

Discovery Thoughts....

Growth occurs from the perception of 'positive and negative' experiences. How have experiences influenced your choices?

_____
_____
_____
_____
_____
_____
_____
_____
_____
_____
_____
_____
_____
_____

What learnings have you embodied that you model in new experiences? How does this practice open you to the flow of Universal energy?

_____
_____
_____
_____
_____
_____
_____
_____
_____
_____
_____
_____
_____
_____
_____

How do you hope to expand with further development and experiences?

_____
_____
_____
_____

_____
_____
_____
_____
_____
_____
_____
_____

Affirmation: I embrace all learning opportunities. I grow and expand with confidence.
Please add an affirmative thought to continue your flow of positive energy.
*I.....*_____

Growth / Maturity

~ Maybe being oneself is always an acquired taste ~
Patricia Hampl
American memoirist, writer and educator

Human development is an innate process of evolution and maturation which crosses all dimensions of life: Ethereal, Mind, Body, Spirit, and Transition. These processes uniquely differentiate us from all other people, as individual beings of Light in human form.

Stages of development proceed in a sequential pattern and include qualitative and quantitative changes in verbal acuity, cognitive aptitude, behavior, dexterity, coordination, processing, and independence. Each of these is characterized by specific milestones that correlate with our abilities, needs, intentions and goals.

Each of us grows at our own pace and attains specific levels of functioning when we are physically, mentally and emotionally ready. Our experiences and proficiency can motivate us to move forward, gaining confidence and independence.

The ability to interpret information increases as the ability of the mind grows multidimensionally. Interpretation can be based on experiences, personal preferences, learnings, opinions, and things imagined or created. Underlying our reasoning is an expanding concept of truth; in ourselves, others, and the world at any given moment in time. Interpretation is situational, meaning that it relies on what we are able to grasp with the resources we currently have. Interpretation adds certainty to our beliefs.

~ Out of every crisis comes the chance to be reborn, to reconceive ourselves as individuals, to choose the kind of change that will help us to grow and to fulfill ourselves more completely ~
Nena O'Neill
Author

Our journey includes the development and expansion of our belief system and exploring the purpose of our existence. Questions arise as well as conflicts. We desire to know more but know that our questions may violate the rules and premises engrained in us in childhood and years of education. Growth relies on openness and acceptance of change and belief in the evolution of ourselves and humanity for the greatest good of all.

Discovery Thoughts...

Thoughts are influenced by many experiences and beliefs. What influences your thinking?

_____
_____
_____
_____
_____
_____
_____
_____
_____
_____
_____
_____

How do perceptions influence your choices?

_____
_____
_____
_____
_____
_____
_____
_____
_____
_____
_____
_____

Affirmation: I am alive in the truth of the present. I embrace growth through change.
Please add an affirmative thought to continue your flow of positive energy.
*I....*_____

Living in Spiritual Grace

~ And reach for our lives... for all life...
deep into the cosmos that is our own souls ~
Sonia Johnson
American feminist activist and writer

A sanctuary is a place of repose and refuge, a place of peace. In the physical world it can be associated with the holiest part of a temple or church, a sacred space. Likewise the sanctuary of your soul brings you closest to your spirit, the higher power that lives within you.

A spiritual relationship is one of freedom; to be your authentic self, to create all you desire, to love without limits, and to be one in unity. One as all.

~Gardening is an instrument of Grace~
Mary Sarton
American poet and novelist

In your soul garden life appears as unimaginable beauty. Everything you have ever needed or imagined exists along your soul's pathway. It's magnificence glows from the splendor of blooms to the most delicate petal flushed with dew. You are surrounded in a world of flourishing life, the seeds of your lifetimes. From the Tree of Life, paths weave through memories, experiences, and emotions. You may wander as you choose, observing and contemplating the years that have produced them, the path you are now walking, and the future you aspire to.

~When the soul wishes to experience something she throws an image of
the experience out before her and enters into her own image ~
Meister Eckhart
German theologian, philosopher, and mystic

Your soul garden is a place of multidimensional capability, a quantum field where all there is can be, and all that is, is as it was meant to be. You are meant to create abundance for yourself and others, in nature and within the earthly plane. Using the energy within you, proportional in magnitude to the vibrational frequency it represents, you continue to create your life through your thoughts and actions. The higher the frequency of your vibrational energy the more love and positivity you project. Higher vibrational energy increases the ability to live in balance and alignment.

Discovery Thoughts...
Imagine you are standing in your soul garden. How do you feel spiritually connected?

_____

_____

_____

_____

_____
_____
_____
_____
_____
_____
_____
_____
_____

The high frequency of our vibrational energy gives us multidimensional capabilities. Using this energy source, what would you create?

_____
_____
_____
_____
_____
_____
_____
_____
_____
_____
_____
_____
_____
_____
_____
_____

Affirmation: I am a sacred instrument of spiritual energy. I create love and abundance.
Please add an affirmative thought to continue your flow of positive energy.
I....._____

CHAPTER 6

Bourgeoning Life

*~ And the day came when the risk (it took) to remain tight in the
bud was more painful than the risk it took to blossom ~*
Anais Nin
French-Cuban American diarist and novelist

All growth is a process of expansion. Consider the factors needed to become a flower in bloom. We plant a seed, either consciously or subconsciously, which germinates. The shell, its protection, must be exposed to earth, water, air, and the energy of the sun. In response, the shell must open to reveal its contents and allow the seed to respond, to create roots. As roots grow they anchor into the ground shedding their seed covering and providing a channel for energy from the plant to ground back into the earth. A sprout rises up from the seed seeking light. The seed is new life, expanding above and below.

Sprouts gain strength and capacity to become seedlings, then grow as shoots with stems and leaves that are able to be identified through their unique characteristics as specific types of plants. Stems grow longer, stronger, and advance in the three-process Helix of Growth: Development, Experience and Expansion.

~ The growth of understanding follows an ascending spiral rather than a straight line ~
Joanna Field
British author and psychoanalyst

Based on the specificity of the plant there are external and internal factors that determine and influence what it will produce. If the plant is to bloom, a bud will form at the tip of the seedling wrapped in protective leaf coverings. The bud is encased to ensure it will have optimum time to develop and to be protected in its vulnerable state. This is a state which parallels our own uniqueness waiting to open to our authenticity; the person you are and the person you are becoming.

Progressive stages of development and the warmth of light signal a time for the bud to begin its revelation. In circular succession, protective leaves peel back and tender petals begin to separate from the hull. With every advancement more of the bloom becomes fully visible. It is a phase of maturity and an expression of courage. In this brief time of opening, its beauty and fragrance permeates the air. The bloom exposes itself to nature; bees, butterflies, and birds to fulfill its purpose of nourishing the garden. Its full expansion is a stage of enlightenment.

Seedlings

~ Once you are real you can't become unreal again. It lasts for always ~
Margery Williams
British – American author, children's books

We choose the seeds we plant. As the seedling grows it makes itself more visible, understanding that all is finely orchestrated in Divine Order and Timing. Growth activates consciousness and increases our capacity to understand ourselves, our needs, and our choices.

A parallel process arises from the stems with the emergence of *Leaves of Progression*, the outward signs of the outcomes of our stages of growth. Knowledge, comprehension, beliefs, self-worth, confidence, consciousness, independence, and maturity are examples of outcomes we can experience.

There are nine types of seedling growth that describe our actionizing "stem" phases. Each have associated sub categories that further define their purpose.

As you read through these lists, consider how these actionizing elements are incorporated into your growth. Consider what you have achieved and embodied into your life processes to be ignited again as you replant. Positive life skills facilitate optimum growth and wellbeing.

~ We are the flow, we are the ebb. We are the weavers, we are the web ~
Shekinah Mountain Water
Musician, author, teacher

Sensing
Hearing, Feeling, Seeing, Tasting, Smelling

Developing
Emerging, Growing, Progressing, Becoming
Standing, Maturing, Expanding
Enlightening, Transitioning

Communicating
Speaking, Asking, Expressing, Requesting, Describing, Questioning, Listening
Conversing, Elaborating, Negotiating, Story Telling, Vibrating

Living
Being, Belonging, Experiencing, Embracing, Releasing, Freeing, Rejoicing
Pursuing, Initiating, Actionizing, Strengthening, Receiving, Motivating
Energizing, Relating, Exploring, Discovering

Thinking
Feeling, Interpreting, Contemplating, Questioning, Learning, Knowing
Processing, Assessing, Evaluating, Organizing, Perceiving, Filtering, Choosing

Creating
Hoping, Desiring, Dreaming, Envisioning, Designing, Projecting
Manifesting, Illuminating, Mirroring, Germinating

Being of Service
Caring, Helping, Aiding, Giving, Sharing, Nurturing
Mentoring, Inspiring, Supporting, Loving

Praying
Meditating, Thanking, Forgiving, Accepting
Allowing, Believing, Communing, Blessing

Integrating
Absorbing, Connecting, Coordinating, Balancing, Surrendering
Inner Child, Higher Self
Assimilating, Transcending, Ascending, Intuiting

~ *It's when we're given choice that we sit with the Gods and design ourselves* ~
Dorothy Gilman
Author, novelist

Seedlings are the actionizing elements of our life that we have chosen to cultivate. Each assists us in continuing growth processes to live more fully and further develop our uniqueness as Divine Beings of Light and Love.

Discovery Thoughts...

Choose a seedling category and describe how you have grown and matured in this area of your life.

_____
_____
_____
_____
_____
_____
_____
_____
_____
_____
_____
_____

The Helix of Growth progresses by development, experience and expansion. In reflecting on your life, what expansive learnings were pivotal in leading you to the present ?

_____
_____
_____
_____
_____
_____
_____
_____
_____
_____
_____
_____
_____
_____

Leaves of progression are the outcomes of your experiences. What outcomes do you wish to manifest from your experiences?

_____
_____
_____
_____

_____

_____

_____

_____

_____

_____

_____

_____

_____

_____

Affirmation: My life offers me unlimited experiences and manifested outcomes.
Joy surrounds me!
Please add an affirmative thought to continue your flow of positive energy.
*I.....*_____

"I like to think of thoughts as living blossoms borne by the human tree."
James Douglas
American leader

BIRD OF PARADISE
Surrender

CHRYSANTHEMUM
Truth

LAVENDER ROSE
Love

VERBENA
Spirituality

PURPLE IRIS
Intuition

PASSION FLOWER
Faith

Blossoms

~ Every flower is a soul blossoming in nature ~
Gerard De Nerval
French poet, essayist, and translator

We are beings of Divine Light cultivating our lives and sharing the blossoms that come forth. Buds emerge comprised of colorful and brilliant *Petals of Assimilation*, each one a symbol of our journey. Each color a symbol of spiritual energy that encourages, promotes and gives sustenance to garden life. We bloom with varying levels of attainment, but always with visible signs of purpose and hope.

When a flower blooms, unfolding its petals to reveal its heart, it is the highest level of its life cycle. Petals surround the blossom in circular patterns, continuing to affix themselves through connection to the core while exposing the inner most place of source and vulnerability.

One plant may have several blossoms that open all at once or at separate times. Many plants in the garden can also yield the same types of blossoms. [occurring at different times in life, and for different reasons] Each blossom representing what you ultimately create at any given time.

There are three stages of blossoming: Intention, Manifestation, and Realization.
The Bud is representative of intention, the desire to become a flower in bloom.
The Petals are products of manifestation, thought in a materialized form.
The Blossom is the realization of a discovery, maturity, or truth. Each blossom creates seeds that will spread their goodness and kindness and create again.

~ Bloom where you're planted ~
Mary Engelbrett
Author, artist

There are six types of blossoms, the culmination of multiple openings of the petals of assimilation. Each blossom is listed below with corresponding petals of assimilation.

Truth
Accuracy, Correctness, Validity, Factuality
Integrity, Wholeness, Sincerity, Authenticity
Honesty, Candor, Principle, Certainty
Sincerity, Openness, Forthrightness

Love
Attachment, Security, Affection, Belonging
Joy, Benevolence, Embrace/Release
Compassion, Sympathy, Self-esteem, Love of self
Devotion, Agape, Adoration, Gratitude, Kindness, Charity
Giving, Philanthropy, Altruism

Faith
Belief, Ideology, Interpretation, Opinion, Sentiment
Reliance, Obedience, Commitment, Dedication, Loyalty
Conviction, Assurance, Optimism, Confidence, Credence

Spirituality
Karma, Chakras, Higher Calling
Adoration, Inspiration, Higher Self
I AM, Soul Purpose, Life Path
One as Whole, One with Spirit

Intuition
Inherent, Innate
Instinct, Visceral, Sensitivity
Perception, Insight, Premonition
Vibration, Deja – Vu, Clairvoyant, Visionary
Third Eye

Surrender
Allowing, Openness, Sacrifice, Capitulation
Acceptance, Service, Freedom, Concede, Relent
Submit, Acquiesce, Relinquish, Yield

> *~ God is in the details ~*
> Ludwig Mies Vander Rohe
> German – American architect

Blossoms are the product of our purposeful intention, manifestation and realization. They complete stages of growth cycles and provide a visual representation of our creation and journey. Blossoms bring beauty and richness to the garden, increase our understanding of individualization, and with kindness and vulnerability, seek to support other life.

Discovery Thoughts...
Choose a Blossom category in which you have experienced blooming. Describe that growth and what it represented to you.

_____
_____
_____
_____
_____
_____
_____
_____
_____

_____

_____

_____

_____

_____

_____

Affirmation: I am beautiful. My life blooms with my creativity.
Please add an affirmative thought to continue your flow of positive energy.
I...._____

Sun and Shade plants

> ~ *I have a little shadow that goes in and out with me, And what*
> *can be the use of [her] is more than I can see* ~
> Robert Louis Stevenson
> Scottish novelist, poet, and travel writer

All plants have purpose. In our garden, as in our lives, we need balance, and what we perceive as opposites assists us in gaining equilibrium. Like night and day, both sun and shade plants complete the natural order of things.

Thriving in the shade is not a negative trait. Roots will always gravitate to the Light, acquiring additional energy to use for the highest good, and to send nourishing energy back to earth. We are also drawn to the Light and the positivity in the world, guided by our inner voice and the conviction of values and beliefs.

> ~ *Flowers grow out of dark moments* ~
> Corita Kent
> Catholic nun, artist and educator

Shadow plants offer a different perspective and allow us to look at life with more discrimination. Experiences we have had that contained negativity, anger, and jealousy, ultimately promoted learning and establishment of new roots. When we evaluate what is best for our growth, we give plants recognition for the purposes they have and have had in increasing our awareness to make changes. Through the growth of our shadow plants we are better able to understand the life processes of others with compassion and empathy.

Things we see in a shadow/negative light reflect back to us; in how we view and judge others and ourselves. Dr. Wayne Dyer expresses this beautifully when he tells us "Remember the truth I've written about many times: *You do not attract what you want; you attract what you are.*"

It is the shadow side that assists you in finding your voice and living authentically.

Love your shadow unconditionally. Love yourself fully for who you truly are. In striving for perfection we may reject unique aspects of ourselves. When you love and accept your shadow side, you can reclaim your gifts to be one with all.

Discovery Thoughts...

What characteristics do you see in your shade plants? How do you incorporate them into the garden?

_____

_____

_____

_____

_____

_____

_____

_____

_____

_____

_____

_____

_____

_____

_____

_____

_____

Affirmation: I love myself fully and unconditionally. I give myself Divine Love.
Please add an affirmative thought to continue your flow of positive energy.
*I.....*_____

CHAPTER 7

The Spiritual Gardener

~ *Good gardening is very simple, really.*
You just have to learn to think like a plant ~
Barbara Damrosch
Writer, horticulturalist

Growth is a natural order of life. If we look to nature as an example, growth will still occur even when nothing is done to promote it. Nature seeks to thrive and rebalance.

Seasons

~ *There is no season such delight can bring*
as summer, autumn, winter, and spring ~
William Browne
English pastoral poet

Every season has a primary purpose and responsibility in the garden and they represent time to be used in a constructive way. They are cyclic in sequences that allow natural flow into the next progression of life. Seasons parallel human processes of growth: rest, rebirth, expand, and reap.

<u>Winter</u> is a time of dormancy. Our plants sleep in the cold under the silent earth. We rest to clear our minds, heal our bodies and hearts, and replenish the soil, our foundation for growth.

<u>Spring</u> is a time of rebirth. We absorb increasing amounts of Light to nourish us and begin processes of new growth. We stir and stretch and plan, designing new life through manifestation.

<u>Summer</u> is a time of beauty, bounty, productivity, and gratitude. We encircle ourselves in perpetual energy and move forward on our soul path. We utilize what is surrounding us to expand to our fullest dimension.

<u>And in the Fall</u> we rejoice in the abundance of the harvest. There is transformation in us and our garden with visible changes in appearance and character. We celebrate a new level of maturity, and take time to prepare again for winter to sustain all life.

All four seasons promote our wellbeing and future growth. Being aware of their purpose allows us to be present to the day and maximize its usefulness and potential.

Discovery Thoughts...
Knowing that nature seeks to thrive and rebalance, how do you use each season to rest, rebirth, expand and reap?

_____
_____
_____
_____
_____
_____
_____
_____
_____
_____
_____
_____
_____
_____
_____

Affirmation: I am one with all cycles of life. Nature restores my energy and balance.
Please add an affirmative thought to continue your flow of positive energy.
*I....*_____

Nourishment

> ~ *You sent out beyond your recall,*
> *go to the limits of your longing.*
> *Embody me* ~
> Rainer Maria Rilke
> Austrian poet and novelist

All living things require nourishment to promote multi-dimensional growth; physically, mentally, emotionally, and spiritually. Certain nutrients also assist us in protection, immunity, and optimizing wellbeing.

Selfcare and self-nurturance is love we give ourselves that fosters love for others. Releasing negativity and criticism builds trust, confidence, and relationships. The act of planting seeds is the giving of life.

Being genuine is an act of faith that nourishes our whole being. It requires that our truth be in alignment with our higher self, without attachment to ego or fear. To be genuine requires courage, the courage to know that we are unique for a reason, for a purpose, and that we are meant to share our talents and spirit. Courage strengthens us to be willing to discover the depth of ourselves and fulfill life purpose.

When we ask for blessings upon ourselves and others, upon all life, we project positive energy with love and generosity. Blessings are garden fertilizer. Blessings nourish with intent to bring goodness forward in the world.

Discovery Thoughts...

Pause a moment to breathe in and align with your Higher Self. What blessing would you send to yourself today? What blessing would you send out into the world?

_____

_____

_____

_____

_____

_____

_____

_____

_____

_____

_____

_____

_____

_____

_____

Affirmation: I am a blessing to life. Blessings nourish me with positivity and generosity. *Please add an affirmative thought to continue your flow of positive energy.*
I....._____

Energy

~ *For me, I know of nothing else but miracles* ~
Walt Whitman
American poet, essayist, and journalist

Dynamic energy abounds in life and bathes the soul garden. Sunlight, moonlight, starlight; spiritual guidance, cosmic alignment, and the energy of the multidimensions of the Universe transmit energy in the form of vibrations. Our seeds and bodies draw this energy inward to transform ourselves. As human beings we absorb energy through physical pathways, chakra energy flow, and our heart connection to soul. Energetic connection is meant to elevate us, connecting mind~body~spirit as one.

Dreams are messages through the subconscious. Ideas and feelings in the conscious mind can surface in dreams, bringing them to a place where we feel safe and secure to explore them. They may be desires of the heart or spiritual messages. Dreams can be discoveries in motion,

indicating a time of newness, transition and change. During subconscious sleep we are open for thoughts to come forward and float through us in channeled multidimensional space.

Manifestation is our ability to create in the physical world using the energy of spirit and intention. It is based on the Law of Attraction and the belief that directed thoughts and words seek connection with similar entities, with form. Manifestation is envisioning what you desire followed through with affirmative action steps that enable life forces to guide you.

Trust your intuition and your power over the illusions of the physical world. The abilities to create on the earthly plane and in your soul garden are the energetic alignment of conscious choice and soul purpose.

~ *Destiny is the push of our instincts to the pull of our purpose* ~
T. D. Jakes
Bishop, author, and filmmaker

Dynamic energy comes forward to assist us in sensing what is beyond our normal comprehension. Through its connection we are able to explore and utilize the depth of power it presents to us.

Discovery Thoughts...
How do you use the energy of manifestation to create what you desire in life?

_____
_____
_____
_____
_____
_____
_____
_____
_____
_____
_____
_____
_____
_____
_____

Affirmation: I am guided through the wisdom of Spirit. I manifest the life I desire.
Please add an affirmative thought to continue your flow of positive energy.
*I.....*_____

Weeding

~ A heart that has been broken and seen pain, reveals
within it, a crack that allows more light in ~
Madisyn Taylor
Author, cofounder DailyOM

Every garden requires weeding, certainly once a year or perhaps more often with the frequent changes that occur in life. Neglecting your weeding grows a garden out of control, where being able to distinguish between plants [that you want] and weeds [that you do not need] becomes more difficult.

Spring, summer, and fall provide opportunities to move through your soul garden with careful eyes and hands to keep all the "beds" in order. Winter allows time for reflection and assessing the past fruitful seasons of growth. Even in winter, reviewing and planning for spring can reveal insights and priorities. If left unattended, weeds will invade and crowd other plants, leaving them vulnerable to disease and garden pests.

Weeding is a process of clearing and releasing. It requires conscious effort to look carefully at the true weeds in your life, things that no longer serve you, things that are no longer in balance with who you have become: old habits, beliefs, negativity, judgments, neglect, guilt, and anger. This is your opportunity to review their growth and make conscious changes.

Sometimes we attach to other people's negative energy and absorb it. Once absorbed it conflicts with our consciousness and ability to balance. This energy can also produce weeds in the garden. Weeding is clearing old energy, energy that hampers progress in life and on your soul path.

Look into your soul garden as an observer and choose where you want to focus. Remember that at one time most weeds were plants with flowers blooming in their own right. They had purpose in your life. You learned from them.

You may not like a particular plant but the question is why? Plants can be trimmed, moved to different areas, and tended to differently to promote new growth.

Through experiences we sense, feel, perceive, and create mental snapshots. We store them. The meaning we have attached to memories can greatly affect how we live in the present. Expectations of what will occur in the future (like fond memories associated with childhood holidays) may far exceed the reality of what was in the past, and the past can never be recreated in the present. The world is different. We have become different. Knowing that nothing is the same, we can gratefully allow everything to be new. Let your mind be open.

~ The past is never where you think you left it ~
Katherine Anne Porter
Journalist, novelist, political activist

Do not allow a negative experiences to overtake the garden. Weeds grow in a moment of time in conjunction with specific circumstances and are not reflective of the garden as a whole. Negativity, the voice of the ego, is seen in fear, judgments, anger, resentment, and arrogance. When negativity grows in the garden it chokes other plants at their roots.

Ego and arrogance weeds try to control you, wanting you to remain chained to lower-self energies. Anger, resentment and judgment weeds try to stifle you, blunting your potential. Thorns, briars, and prickle weeds try to hurt you, subordinating you to give them power.

All weeds can be used as compost, grounding energy back into the earth. As you tend your garden and create your compost beds, remember to bless their worth as they have brought you to this place of higher awareness. Bless their purpose to fertilize new soil with renewed energy.

> ~ *True satisfaction with one's life is an acceptance of what is, continuing to prepare for what can be, while letting go of what we thought needed to be* ~
> Anne Wilson Schaef
> Clinical psychologist and author

Weeding is the conscious releasing of the past to promote new growth. Careful attention to what you wish to create allows for discernment in choosing what no longer serves you. With respect for their role in promoting experiences and learnings, we bless the weeds in our garden and return them to the earth.

Discovery Thoughts...
What weeds have you consciously removed from your Soul Garden?

_____
_____
_____
_____
_____
_____
_____
_____
_____
_____
_____
_____
_____

Affirmation: I release all that no longer serves me.
I ground life energy back into the earth.
Please add an affirmative thought to continue your flow of positive energy.
*I....*_____

84

"Help us to be ever faithful gardeners of the spirit, who know that without darkness nothing comes to birth, and without light nothing flowers."
May Sarton
Poet and novelist

Transplantation/Propagation

~What we do to survive is often different from what we need to do in order to live...
The way to freedom often lies through the open heart ~
Naomi Remen, M.D.
Author, pioneer of holistic mind/body medicine

There are two processes in the garden which seek to create new life by moving or using part of the existing plant to create new growth: transplantation and propagation. Both processes are intended to preserve the energy of the existing plant.

Transplantation shifts the plant body to a similar but more beneficial environment within its setting or removes it completely from the soil to relocate it. Careful consideration should be given to the phase of growth a plant is in before it is transplanted, remembering that grounded energy from the roots will always remain in the earth.

Transplantation can be seen in the physical world when one chooses a new job or career. Our work life is reflective of our desire to contribute and be of benefit to the world. When we accept new work we are exchanging environments, expectations, and opportunities for new growth.

Propagation seeks to multiply the attributes of the plant by direct use of the plant body rather than using its seeds. Spiritually, propagation is giving of the self, an act of service. Propagation always creates new opportunity for growth.

Propagation is akin to changes in life circumstances wherein you retain part of you as you are in the present while giving another part to a higher purpose. Examples of this would be marriage or divorce, or taking vows when joining a convent. You are beginning anew while still residing in the garden as before.

~ Each morning we are born again. What we do today is what matters most ~
Buddha
Spiritual teacher, philosopher

The Soul Garden offers us opportunities to recreate our lives. Through transplantation and propagation we preserve the energy of our initial seeds and intentions and are able to begin anew.

Discovery Thoughts...

Think of an experience in your life in which you transplanted or propagated yourself.

What did you create in the new environment?

_____

_____

_____

_____

_____
_____
_____
_____
_____
_____
_____
_____
_____

How would you choose to transform yourself?

_____
_____
_____
_____
_____
_____
_____
_____
_____
_____
_____
_____
_____
_____

Affirmation: I create new growth with change. I multiply that which I divide.
Please add an affirmative thought to continue your flow of positive energy.
*I.....*_____

CHAPTER 8

Healing

~ To one who waits, all things reveal themselves, so long as you have the courage not to deny in the darkness what you have seen in the Light ~
Coventry Patmore
British poet and art critic

Healing is a continuous process of discovery, recovery, change and opportunity. We heal physically, mentally and spiritually from the inside, the Higher Self, to affect our outer aspects. Our wellbeing depends on the alignment of the mind~body~spirit.

Emotions [sensing] create feelings arising from perceptions and interpretations of the mind. They are an expression of being human, neither good nor bad. While we process emotions and determine responses, the mind gains power in whatever it dwells on. The body mimics the mind's focus by displaying behaviors, attitudes, and body image that reflects its disposition. Episodes of anger, sadness, or frustration are rooted in emotion. Depression is a state of dwelling that outwardly presents the dark characteristics of its focus.

Self-esteem, self-worth and authenticity are important to overall health and healing.

What we believe about ourselves creates an image of who we are. Own and accept your present life as it is. Know that you can continue to create that which you desire and desire to be. Empower yourself to create the change you wish to embody.

Believe in yourself and the holy creation that you are. Holy means sacred. Treat yourself as the sacred being you are.

Healing as a Process

~ Sometimes a person has to go back, really back – to have a sense, and understanding of all that's gone to make them – before they can go forward ~
Paule Marshall
Author

In times of misalignment you have veered off your life path. In essence, there are aspects of you that are lost. Healing is change and change is a process. Obstacles and forces of resistance are meant to be messages. Recurring patterns and experiences serve to guide you to unfinished issues, encouraging you to explore them once more. Be conscious of your truth and any deviations from it. Deviations are illusions rising from ego mind.

Unresolved negative feelings can become deeply rooted and eventually present as physical symptoms or a physical problem. Reflection allows you to observe the soul garden and understand where healing is needed. All outward signs of illness in the physical plane have a corresponding inward source.

In order to truly heal, the mind~body~spirit needs to be simultaneously cared for and nurtured in two planes of existence, the earthly and the spiritual. The body and mind in the earthly plane create outcome oriented healing by monitoring and initiating physiological and psychological responses to regain physical homeostasis. These create changes in body processes. Physical symptoms are indications of these changes and guide us to make adjustments and seek interventions that are required for health.

On the spiritual plane, the spiritual-self desires to share the wisdom of the Higher Self.

It requires that the mind be open, listen, and allow the current of healing thoughts to come forward. Imagine a flow of sacred water, a stream, arising from your higher self and flowing into your body. Feel its soothing sensations as it washes away all aspects of negativity and fear. The stream flows in continuous motion with your thoughts. Healing energy is infinite.

Emotional healing, the healing of the interpretations of the mind inward to the heart, is a delicate process of unveiling and accepting. The wounds of the emotions are personal injuries, embedded on a visceral level. Personal wounds leave scars, scars that need to be reabsorbed where they can be loved as we love ourselves. Scars restrict us from truly living as one within our whole.

The psychiatrist Carl Jung described a "personal unconsciousness" within us that is overridden with feelings, emotions and memories of the past, both light and dark. These creations of the mind implant themselves into our psyche and can be triggered to seep back into consciousness as if they were happening anew.

Emotional healing requires that we separate events from emotions. What we remember is the story. What we felt is the emotional response. Releasing is a process of consciously emptying the "personal unconsciousness" to fill it with the goodness that you are and desire. Fear becomes trust, anger embraces love. Be willing to delete the story and the memories of the event and other people's actions; what you cannot change. Your present feelings, not the past, are the key to regaining personal power.

Whatever we feel is a legitimate response of the wounded self. Like fight or flight, we make instantaneous decisions to react, then assess and re-evaluate our true feelings later. There is no magic band aid that will take away the pain of deep wounds; we are left to uncover the rawness and work towards regaining balance, alignment and wholeness. The mind is a wizard of connivance and statements like "I should have… known better?" grasp at illusions of control. These ego based recriminations bury truth even deeper, and truth and authenticity are the stepping stones to moving forward.

~ Truly it is in the darkness that one finds the light; so when we
are in sorrow, then this light is nearest to all of us ~
Meister Eckhart
German theologian, philosopher, and mystic

As healing expands from within it also traverses ancestral lineage. Previous similar episodes of imbalance will benefit from current therapeutic practices, opening ourselves to recover from the remnants of the past. Current healing can also influence the future by promoting a higher level of functioning through clearer understanding.

Stress creates a condition of fear which brings disruption to our state of wellness. Constantly living in stress is an attempt to incorporate unhealthy patterns into our being and into our lives to preserve something we feel has value. The value we place upon an entity dictates the level of stress we are willing to accept and attempt to manage. Insecurity, low self-esteem, and fear of abandonment may underlie the need to live in stressful environments, believing we are less than others and less than what we expect of ourselves. What is "expected" of ourselves arises from external and internal forces, and creates illusions of the ego mind. Fear is disruptive to all natural processes and prevents us from actualizing our highest self.

Continuously reliving painful memories weakens our spirit and increases vulnerability. Releasing painful memories is therapeutic and healing. Releasing allows us to grow again by creating space in the garden, and giving us opportunity to learn practices which foster wellbeing.

Forgiveness of self and others is a choice of freedom, and essential to our wellbeing. When we judge others we create negativity and blame. The ego feels we have been wronged and expects compensation. By forgiving, an action of the heart, we are accepting of what has occurred as a factual event. We are not condoning it, but choosing instead to repel the burden of its negativity in our life. By choosing to be free, you are choosing to live with Light and Love and in peace and harmony. You are allowing yourself to love fully as is intended.

All experiences, even painful ones, are learning opportunities. What you experienced eventually brought you to the place where you are now. Ask yourself what did you learn? How did you grow? Is there anything remaining that is toxic to your life and future?

~ All we are asked to bear we can bear. That is a law of the spiritual life.
The only hinderance to the working of this law, as of all benign laws, Is fear ~
Elizabeth Goudge
British author of novels, short stories and children's books

Healing is an act of the Higher Self energy seeking to balance and realign mind~body~spirit.

Physical symptoms and problems are messengers guiding us to see patterns and situations for their truth and purpose. Emotional healing, as an extension of the mind, creates a deeper understanding of our sense of self and wholeness. Throughout our lifetimes we desire to experience the freedom of wholeness and release all fear and negativity. Healing requires that the mind be open and allow the flow of the Higher Self thoughts to come forward.

Discovery Thoughts ....

In what areas of your life have you experienced healing?

_____

_____

_____

_____

_____

_____

_____

_____

_____

_____

_____

_____

Emotional healing requires that we empty our "personal unconsciousness". What remains in this aspect of your mind that you wish to release?

_____

_____

_____

_____

_____

_____

_____

_____

_____

_____

_____

_____

_____

_____

_____

_____

What does forgiveness mean to you? Is there anything in your life you feel needs forgiveness?

_____

_____

_____

_____
_____
_____
_____
_____
_____
_____
_____
_____
_____

Affirmation: I embody the flow of Higher Self energy. I live in health and wholeness.
Please add an affirmative thought to continue your flow of positive energy.
*I.......*_____

"Love one another and help others to rise to the higher levels, simply by pouring out love.
Love is infectious and the greatest healing energy."
Sai Baba
Indian spiritual master

Energetic Healing

~ The child is an almost universal symbol for the soul's transformation.
The child is whole, not yet divided....
When we would heal the mind....
We ask this child to speak to us ~
Susan Griffin
Philosopher, essayist, and playwright

The natural order of life is to heal and return the mind, body and spirit to a state of balance and alignment. We are in a perpetual course of recalibration. Healing is life and growth nourished at the same time. Unresolved issues with emotional gravity and guilt have a strong magnetic energy attraction and attract situations with the same vibration.

We create higher vibration with positive action, acceptance and love. Prayer, meditation, and being surrounded by nature create higher frequency energy states.

Offer a blessing to all people and situations to assist in healing yourself and others. Ask for Divine Grace. What you project into the world is reflected back to you.

Reiki is energetic healing based on the Japanese methods developed by Dr. Usui from ancient Tibetan texts. Reiki means Universal Life Force – the healing energy of the universe. As the Reiki practitioner's hands move above your body, healing energy flows through your chakra energy centers to promote balance and harmony through all dimensions of your being. Reiki can reveal information that points to areas of your body and mind that are misaligned, and lead you to insightful physical and spiritual discoveries.

The processes of healing require awareness and participation. Envision yourself releasing any pain and illness. Envision a golden white light flowing down through your crown chakra to illuminate you with the goodness and wellness of healing energy. Allow the light to float over you and through you, collecting all fragments of imbalance and washing them away, all the way down your body and through the soles of your feet to ground back to Mother Earth.... Frequently practice seeing this clearing taking place and your healing occurring.

Angelic healing supports you when you ask for Divine intervention. Specific Masters, Archangels, Angels and Guides have guidance over aspects of your life and can be called upon for general assistance in areas of need. Be aware that healing is occurring whether results are palpable to you or not, and give thanks and gratitude for these gifts. Angelic healing is compassionate healing through the heart.

Energetic healing occurs in multiple dimensions on many physical and spiritual planes. It is the flow of positive vibration within us, through us and from us to reestablish alignment and positivity. With the blessings of Divine Grace we open ourselves to vibrational healing energy forces.

Discovery Thoughts ....

How do you incorporate the flow of universal energy into your life?

_____
_____
_____
_____
_____
_____
_____
_____
_____
_____
_____
_____
_____
_____
_____

How does positive energy promote your wellbeing?

_____
_____
_____
_____
_____
_____
_____
_____
_____
_____
_____
_____
_____
_____
_____

Affirmation: I am an open, receptive channel of Divine healing energy.
I give thanks and gratitude for my health and wellness.
Please add an affirmative thought to continue your flow of positive energy
*I.....*_____

Replenishment

~ This is the art of courage: to see things as they are and still believe that the victory lies not with those who avoid the bad, but those who taste, in living awareness, every drop of the good ~
Victoria Lincoln
Author and biographer

As we heal, our mind~body~spirit is replenished from life storms, trauma, emotional gravity and misalignment. Attention to daily practices that assist in maintaining balance help to promote growth and wellness.

Breathing is the movement of air and associated energy in and out of the body and was the first essential activity of our lives as we emerged into the world. Breathing is automatically adjusted by our nervous system to meet physical and psychological demands. In times of stress, exercise, illness, or fear, the rate and depth of breathing is automatically adjusted to deliver more oxygen and/or to release more carbon dioxide. These processes compensate for altered physiological states and work to rebalance our metabolic state. We can learn to adjust our breathing as a method of relaxation, to release thoughts and emotions, and to facilitate meditation. Slow deep breaths are calming and promote realignment as we exhale negativity and fear from within.

Breathing is a wonderful exercise to regain balance. Bring forward that which you desire in your life and breathe out that which does not serve you. Breathe with awareness until you feel a sense of serenity within you. Build your inner strength with its movement and consistency. Focus on components of your abilities which you use to create goodness in the world. Consciously remove all obstacles to your authenticity and truth.

Release any barriers to the flow of energy within you. Resist attachment to the emotions and actions of others and allow them to own and be responsible for their feelings and behaviors.

Maintaining balance and replenishing reserves allows you to connect with who you truly are, one with Higher Self. For you are the blessed incarnation of God's love. Know and understand this as the miracle it is!

Care for yourself in a loving, respectful, compassionate way. Care for your inner child, the part of you that still exists and waits uninhibitedly to play again. Remember how that child encouraged you, supported you, and comforted you. Remember your innocence. Remember that you are born with purpose, the life you have chosen. Open your wings and give flight!

Practice dormancy as a daily replenishment life cycle. Find in each day....

The gift of rest
The gift of silence
The gift of listening in the dark, in the void
The gift of beginning again.....

 100

Spend time in your soul garden. Walk between your plants and blossoms. Notice what you have created and give thanks. State affirmations that reinforce your value and what you want to manifest. Bless yourself and your intentions.

*∼ I will love the light for it shows the way, yet I will endure
the darkness because it shows me the stars ∼*
Og Mandino
American author

Replenishment is a necessary component of nourishment and nurturance. We facilitate this by choosing to rest and reflect, breathing in what we desire and breathing out what we wish to release. By replenishing we create more room in the garden for positivity, love, and spiritual oneness.

Discovery Thoughts ....
How do you replenish yourself each day?

_____
_____
_____
_____
_____
_____
_____
_____
_____
_____
_____
_____
_____
_____

Being playful and imaginative fosters the innocence of our inner child to resurface.
How would you choose to experience the freedom of your inner child again?

_____
_____
_____
_____
_____
_____
_____
_____
_____

_____
_____
_____
_____
_____
_____

Affirmation: I AM freedom and self-empowerment.

I breathe with life's energy.

Please add an affirmative thought to continue your flow of positive energy

I...._____

CHAPTER 9

Life Paths

Pathways

> ~ *Sometime in your life you will go on a journey.*
> *It will be the longest journey you have ever taken.*
> *It is the journey to find yourself* ~
> Katherine Sharp
> Librarian and historian

You are on a spiritual journey and your life is filled with endless possibility.

Our minds envision opportunities from which we create limitless abundance, health, and happiness. Life is a path and our path is a process of continuous growth. All experiences provide learning and expansion. We cannot go backward to eliminate an outcome, but we can retrace our steps to gain a broader understanding and a higher perspective. Seeing all paths through the eyes of Divine Love is the highest perspective we can hold.

The Soul Garden grows outward from the Tree of Life lined by circular pathways, each representing a phase of life. All paths are connected by thought and intention.

In walking our paths we consciously proceed in a direction, each step building upon all others. Each day has purpose in our life. Destinations evolve and there are side roads, stopping points, and detours. No matter where we have traveled we are not far from our Tree of Life, our centering point. All paths lead us back to where we need to be.

The garden is a Quantum field in which anything can be produced with manifested energy. There is absence of measured time and unlimited space. As you walk in reflection, choose to consciously step forward. Pathways join the gardens of our life's journeys. Walk in cadence to the mantra: relax, release, receive, replenish.

Discovery Thoughts ....

Visualize walking your life paths in the Soul Garden. How has one path led to the other? How have these paths brought you to the place where you are now?

_____
_____
_____
_____
_____

_____
_____
_____
_____
_____
_____
_____
_____
_____
_____

Affirmation: My journey is spiritually guided. Divine Light illuminates my soul path.
Please add an affirmative thought to continue your flow of positive energy
*I.....*_____

"We cannot stop the winter or the summer from coming. We cannot stop the spring or the fall or make them other than they are. They are gifts from the Universe that we cannot refuse. But we can choose what we will contribute to life when each arrives."
Gary Zukav
American spiritual teacher, author

Soul Purpose

*~ The two most important days of your life are the day you
were born and the day you find out why ~*
Mark Twain
Writer, humorist, and publisher

There is no specific age at which we begin to understand where we belong in the world, though we begin to ask relevant questions in early years. Some of us hear a higher calling coming from a place where we are meant to be, to be of service for the greater good. Others will move forward believing they are well "suited" for a career/position or may accept it out of convenience or sense of duty. Along life's pathway we will continue to search, ask for assistance, and receive guidance. Listening to inner voice, the Higher Self, is critical to finding soul purpose.

Traditionally teenage years are adventurous and a time of discovery. Lessons learned have lasting impact on what we believe about the world, ourselves and others. As we grow, experience, and expand we can restructure, building upon previous foundations and strengthening the knowledge of who we truly are. In our garden we seed new plants that are heartier and more "disease resistant" to promote optimal new growth and wellbeing.

Messages from spirit guide us in Divine Order and Divine Timing. These communications come through prayer, meditation, mentors, and universal laws. They ask us to extend ourselves and do something *more*, something beyond our current reach.

Hearing these messages we then choose next steps:

- To go forward in faith and promise to fulfill our soul's purpose
- To remain uncomfortable in our present surroundings
- To revert to previous thinking, familiar obstacles that did not fulfill or serve us

How do we know what is our soul's purpose? From thoughts come answers. From possibilities come openings. Soul purpose is a process of discovery on life's journey. By allowing opportunities and change to come into our life we open ourselves to their gifts. Connect with your Higher Self. Listen to your intuition and let your heart speak to you.

*~ The journey of enlightenment is a journey of the mind:
from a focus on the body to a focus on the spirit, from a limited sense of self to an unlimited
sense of self, from a sense of separateness to a sense of unity with all things ~*
Marianne Williamson
American author and spiritual leader

Imagine that you are looking at yourself from two perspectives, above and below. From above you are your Higher Self, seeing your spiritual gifts, the desires of your heart, and the contributions you have made and want to make in the world. From below, you are an objective

observer. You assess what you do, if you like it or not, and the choices you make each day. Your soul desires to reconcile any differences from above and below.

Ask for universal and Divine guidance, clarity and assistance. Look for signs that reinforce your knowledge of where you belong. Look for wisdom and learnings from the Laws of the Universe and the Spiritual Laws, showing you relationship, order, and attraction. Search for the place where you fully engage your talents and are a positive, honest, compassionate dynamic in service to the greater good. Being urged to do more with your life builds confidence and promotes decisions that are in your best interest.

~ Ask and it shall be given to you; seek and ye shall find;
Knock and it shall be opened unto you ~
Matthew 7:7

Own the decisions you have made while solidifying future choices that align with purpose. Every thought, every step, every choice, is a step forward in becoming, in opening fully.

You are your soul, the truth of who you are.

Discovery Thoughts ....
What you believe is your soul purpose? How are you living that purpose?

_____
_____
_____
_____
_____
_____
_____
_____
_____
_____
_____
_____
_____
_____
_____

Affirmation: I am a Light Worker. I bring greater good into the world.
Please add an affirmative thought to continue your flow of positive energy
*I.....*_____

Soul Path

~ There is only one journey. Going inside yourself ~
Rainer Maria Rilke
Austrian poet and novelist

Your soul path is all the pathways you walk, have walked and will walk. Everything is embedded in the steps you take.

Our earthly lives are lived in cycles of Divine Order: birth, growth, death, and rebirth. These are seen repeated in the plants we grow in the soul garden. With deep roots we emerge again, to bloom again, to seed again.

There is purpose in all lives, the spiritual being in physical form. We come to discover, learn, and create more goodness and kindness in the world. We are urged by experiences to search and live an expanded life, embracing all that is.

*~ I slept and dreamt that life was joy. I awoke and saw that life
was service. I acted, and behold, service was joy ~*
Rabindranath Tagore
Bengali poet, writer and composer

We are capable of sensing the needs of others and our universe. We are able to give without expectation of return. To look beyond yourself is a choice of consciousness.

To live with integrity, harmony and authenticity we are asked to:

- Align with our Higher Self and be one with spirit
- Align with our soul's purpose
- Align with our soul's path

Accessing Your Soul Garden

Take in a deep breath, inhaling the fullness of your life....
Your Soul Garden is a place where you belong. It is familiar to you.....

Your Soul Garden is accessible at any time and from any place. Chakra energy pathways act as conduits to allow us to transcend through our heart space to be one with our spiritual self. Divine Energy comes forward as Light to assist you in this journey of discovery.

Walking Your Path

~ The promised land always lies on the other side of the wilderness ~
Havelock Ellis
British physician, writer, and social reformer

Learning to access your garden is a conscious process that requires preparation, time and consistency; in a quiet peaceful atmosphere, in harmony with nature and yourself.

Softly close your eyes and take several comfortable slow deep breaths, in and out, to clear your thoughts. Think of releasing all that is present in your mind. Allow these thoughts to flow from you with exhalation. As you breathe out bless anything that may be troubling you, bless its highest good as you let it go. Allow it to find its own path in the universe.

Keeping your eyes closed, allow your breathing to resume a normal depth and balance as it becomes slower and more shallow. Your mind is continuing to clear and sensations flow to you in the space you have created. You are aware from a distance that your body is breathing in what you need and giving out what no longer serves you. Open all of your being with immense gratitude.

Your body continues to breathe naturally as you connect with the energy flowing through you. Visualize yourself standing somewhere. Maybe a field or a sandy beach, standing barefoot firmly on the ground, connecting with the earth. And as you are standing there breathing in, you feel the energy and vibration of the earth, travelling all the way up your legs, to your back.... Coming in through the lower chakras and up to the root, the sacral, the solar plexus.... In its flowing warmth. You breathe the flow of that energy higher to your chest and heart chakra, anchoring earth's energy into your heart.

And now, feel the energy of the higher realm, the heavenly realm, coming down through your higher chakras, coming down into your crown, connecting you to the Divine Light of Spirit.

The illumination envelopes you, knowing it is you, eternal you. You who have travelled through time and space to be in this now moment. Know that you are here to bring forth a beautiful message, one with your soul's purpose, as only you can bring forth. In this space know that everything you are and everything you need is contained within the Light of this beautiful radiance inside you.

From the top of your head and through your crown chakra, golden light continues to envelop you with its presence. The light expands downward to the center of your forehead, to the gateway of the 3rd eye and into a white void in which your become emerged and one in Spiritual Light.....

You are the Light moving downward, past your throat chakra, the source of voice and truth, and into your heart to unite with the grounded Light from below....

Breathe in... as you move with the flow of golden light deeper into your heart, dropping down into your heart center as if you have entered an expansive room.

Imagine that golden light glowing, spreading outward through all the dimensions of your being, filling every cell and vessel of your body so you are one energy within the Light..... You are the light that continues to move expansively throughout.

Your heart in its pure golden vibration leads you with the flow of grace, one with spirit, through the door, the door in the back of your heart...

.....and you move across the threshold and out into a beautiful field of green....... bathed in bright white Light... where you become present on a golden pathway.....

and you follow the golden pathway across the field and up a small hill to a magnificent tree, a tree taller than your vision, its branches lifting up into celestial skies. You reach out and touch it's skin and it breathes with you, your energy and it's energy as one source.....

and you see before you beautiful gardens of every plant imaginable. Greens and leaves in patterns; blooms and buds in all colors and heights. Gardens of your making, living forms of your thoughts, experiences and lifetimes. You rise up, rise up into the vapors, one with the Light and the magnificence of you.

> ~ *The eyes of my eyes are opened* ~
> E. E. Cummings
> Poet, author, and playwright

Your journey is a process of loving yourself. Love where you have been, love where you are and love where you will go. Love that you are growing. Love that you are able to mature from your experiences and grow again. Love that by loving yourself you are able to love others for themselves. Love that we are all beings in Divine Light and Love.

Discovery Thoughts....

Open your eyes and breathe in the beauty that surrounds you. Describe yourself and what you see.

_____
_____
_____
_____
_____
_____
_____
_____
_____
_____
_____
_____
_____
_____
_____

What does the Soul Garden mean to you? Listen to your Higher Self. What messages come forward?

_____
_____
_____
_____
_____
_____
_____
_____
_____
_____
_____
_____
_____

Affirmation: I am a sacred journey of discovery, acceptance and love.
Please add an affirmative thought to continue your flow of positive energy
*I.....*_____

"A day dawns, quite like other days; in it a single hour comes, quite like other hours, but in that day and in that hour the chance of a lifetime faces us."
Maltie D. Babcock
American clergyman, author

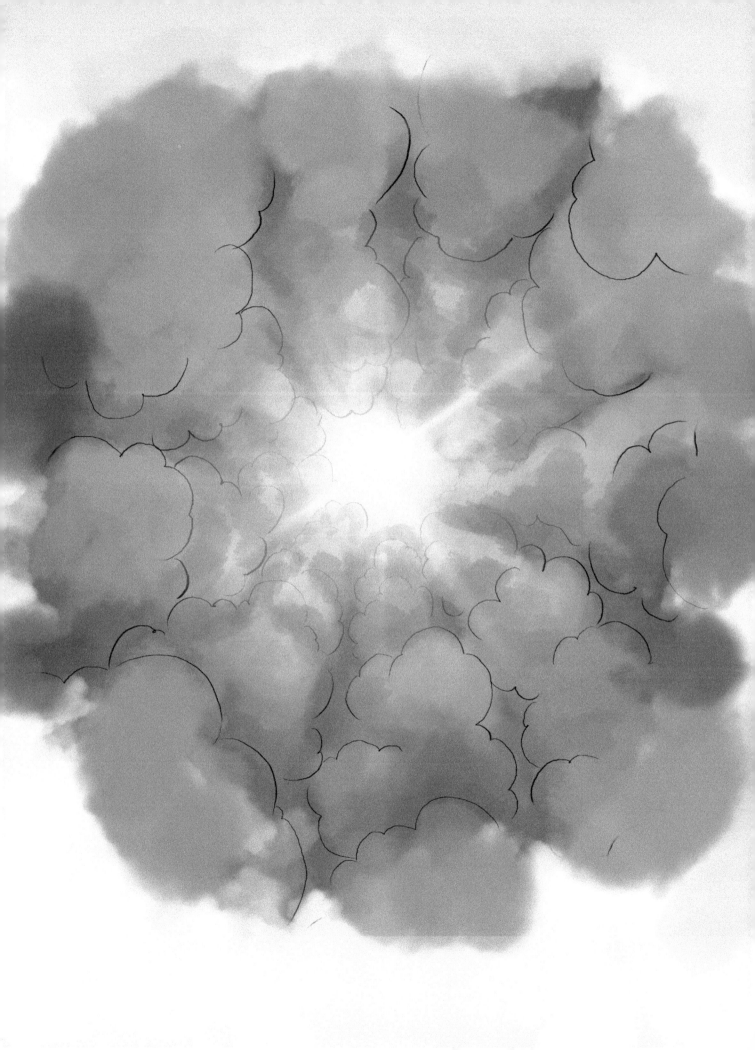

INSPIRATIONAL RESOURCES

A ~

Akashic Wisdom Newsletter by Teri Uktena: teri@spiritwithinus.com

Anam Cara: A Book of Celtic Wisdom by John O'Donohue

Anatomy of the Spirit: The Seven Stages of Power and Healing by Caroline Myss, PH.D.

A Natural History of the Senses by Diane Ackerman

A Return to Love: Reflections on the Principles of a Course in Miracles by Marianne Williamson

A Simple Path by Mother Teresa

A Year of Miracles: Daily Devotions and Reflections by Marianne Williamson

A Year With Thomas Merton: Daily Meditations from His Journals, selected and edited by
    Jonathan Montaldo

B ~

Blessings: Prayers and Declarations for a Heartful Life by Julia Cameron

Bone Sigh Arts, by Terri St Cloud: www.bonesigharts.com

Braving the Wilderness: The Quest for True Belonging and the Courage to Stand Alone by
    Brene Brown, Ph.D., LMSW

C ~ D

Change Your Thoughts – Change Your Life: Living the Wisdom of the Tao by Dr. Wayne W.
    Dyer

Creative Ideas: A Spiritual Compass for Personal Expression by Ernest Holmes

Daring Greatly: How the Courage to be Vulnerable Transforms the Way We live, Love,
Parent, and Lead by Brene Brown, Ph.D., LMSW

Defy Gravity: Healing Beyond the Bounds of Reason by Caroline Myss, Ph.D.

E ~ F

Each day a New Beginning: Daily Meditations for Women by the Editors of the Hazelden
    Foundation

Emmanuel's Book: A Manual for Living Comfortably in the Cosmos by Pat Rodegast and Judith
Stanton

Finding Water: The Art of Perseverance by Julia Cameron

Four Elements: Reflections on Nature by John O'Donohue

H ~

Happiness is the Way: How to Reframe Your Thinking and Work with What YouAlready Have
    to Live the Life of Your Dreams by Dr. Wayne W. Dyer

Heart Steps: Prayers and Declarations for a Creative Life by Julia Cameron

Heart Thoughts: A Treasury of inner Wisdom by Louise Hay

I ~J

Inner Alchemy: The Urban Monk's Guide to Happiness, Health and Vitality by Pedram Shojai, OMD

In the Heart of The World by Mother Teresa

Invisible Acts of Power: Channeling Grace in Your Everyday Life by Caroline Myss Ph.D

Jay Designs Inc, Web Design, Knoxville, Tenn. Janet Edkins, CEO, https://jaydesignsinc.com

K ~L

Kitchen Table Wisdom: Stories that Heal by Rachel Naomi Remen, M.D.

Linde Mills Art, Knoxville, Tenn. Linde Mills, lindemillsart@gmail.com

M ~

Meditations for Women Who Do Too Much by Anne Wilson Schaef

Miracles Now: 108 Life Changing Tools for Less Stress, More Flow, and Finding Your True Purpose by Gabrielle Bernstein

Mornings with the Lord: A year of Uplifting Devotionals to Start Your Day on the Right Path by Doreen Virtue

My Grandfather's Blessings: Stories of Strength, Refuge, and Belonging by Rachel Naomi Remen, M.D.

N ~ O

Native Echoes: Listening to the Spirit of the Land by Kent Nerburn

Natural Health Intuition, Portsmouth, NH. Hilary McCann Crowley, Energy Medicine Practitioner

No Greater Love by Mother Teresa

108 Quotations: A Treasury of Mystical Wisdom by Dhyani Ywahoo

P ~ R

Pocketful of Miracles: Prayers, Meditations, and Affirmations to Nurture Your Spirit Every Day of the Year by Joan Borysenko, Ph.D.

Prayers to the Great Creator: Prayers & Declarations for a Meaningful Life by Julia Cameron

Romancing the Ordinary: A Year of Simple Splendor by Sara Ban Breathnach

S ~

Sacred Rhythms: Arranging Our Lives for Spiritual Transformation by Ruth Haley Barton

7 Paths to God: The Ways of the Mystic by Joan Z. Borysenko, Ph.D.

Simple Abundance: A Daybook of Comfort and Joy by Sarah Ban Breathnach

Simple Truths: Clear and Gentle Guidance on the Big Issues in Life by Kent Nerburn

Small Graces: The Quiet Gifts of Everyday Life by Kent Nerburn

Something More: Excavating Your Authentic Self by Sarah Ban Breathnach

T ~

The Artist's Way: A Spiritual Path to Higher Creativity by Julia Cameron

The Breath of the Soul: Reflections on Prayer by Joan Chittister

The Creation of Health: The Emotional, Psychological, and Spiritual Responses that Promote Health and Healing by Caroline Myss, PH.D. and Norman Shealy, M.D.

The Four Purposes of Life: Finding Meaning and Direction in a Changing World by Dan Millman

The Gift of Change: Spiritual Guidance for Living Your Best Life by Marianne Williamson

The Gifts of Imperfection: Let Go of Who You Think You're Supposed to Be and Embrace Who You Are by Brene Brown, Ph.D., M.M.S.W.

The Gift of Years: Growing Older Gracefully by Joan Chittister

The Holistic Institute of Wellness, Knoxville, Tenn. Carolyn A. Jones, The Energy Architect, www.holisticinstituteofwellness.com

The Laws of Spirit: Simple, Powerful Truths for Making Your Life Work by Dan Millman

The Life You Were Born to Live: A Guide to Finding Your Life Purpose by Dan Millman

The Monastic Way by Joan Chittister, www.monasticway.org

The Power of Intention: Learning To Co-Create Your World Your Way by Dr. Wayne W. Dyer

The Prosperous Heart: Creating a Life of "Enough" by Julia Cameron

The Seven Spiritual Laws of Success: A Practical Guide to the Fulfillment of Your Dreams by Deepak Chopra

The Seven Whispers: A Spiritual Practice for Times Like These by Christina Baldwin

The Universe Has Your Back: Transform Fear to Faith by Gabrielle Bernstein

Through God's Eyes: Finding Peace and Purpose in a Troubled World by Phil Bolsta

Transitions: Prayers and Declarations for a Changing Life by Julia Cameron

V ~ Y

Voices of Our Ancestors: Cherokee Teachings from the Wisdom Fire by Dhyani Ywahoo

Walden by Henry David Thoreau

You Are What You Think: 365 Meditations for Extraordinary Living by Dr. Wayne W. Dyer

ABOUT THE AUTHOR

Sally Gallot-Reeves is a spiritual gardener planting seeds. Her life's work is dedicated to promoting the Highest good for all individuals, animals and nature kingdoms. Communicating through her writing, she reveals her innermost thoughts and feelings to nurture and guide readers to their own discoveries and awareness.

Sally believes compassion, love and acceptance are the foundations to our living in harmony and unity. One as one, one as whole. She credits her years in nursing service to illuminating her heart and mind to the core needs of all people, the sacredness of life, and her dedication to bringing Divine Light and Love into the world.

Her published works include Behind the Open Door: The Book of Light, the story of a highly gifted and telepathic child and her magical adventures navigating a world she doesn't understand; and Between Shifts, a book of vignettes in poetry drawing from her experiences with patients, families and caregivers. She is the author of the Soul Garden Pathway website where she pens daily blessings out into the world that offer hope and insight into life's challenges.

Born in New England, she resides in New Hampshire where she continues her literary work and spiritual life creating sanctuary space for all living things.

You may contact her through her website www.sallygallotreeves.com

CPSIA information can be obtained
at www.ICGtesting.com
Printed in the USA
LVHW071530040921
696975LV00005B/115